THE HUN

"This, I believe, is an important book, a systematic and fearless new look at spirituality in the languages of both the humanities and biology. It is impressive in scholarship and style ... I believe it will stimulate new interest in the subject."

—E. O. WILSON, Harvard University, author
The Creation: An Appeal to Save Life on Earth
Consilience: The Unity of Knowledge

"Carl von Essen mixes the personal, the scientific, and the ecological as he tracks the experiences of nature exemplified by the ways of the hunter, the warrior, the athlete, the mystic, and the scientist. As an angler, physician, scholar, and adventurer, he is uniquely qualified for these explorations. Read and be enlightened!"

—STEPHEN BODIO, author
On the Edge of the Wild: Passions and Pleasures of a Naturalist
Eagle Dreams: Searching for Legends in Wild Mongolia

"A fascinating account of a crucial issue for our species, presented in an intelligent, articulate, and immensely readable way. I feel a close kinship in much of what he says."

—ANTHONY STEVENS, Jungian analyst, author
The Two Million-Year-Old Self ; The Roots of War & Terror

"A significant statement in our present chemical era on the return of the physician to the role of naturalist. To see ourselves through the lens of nature is to see that everything in nature is reflected in the life of the soul. And when we see this, God speaks to us and our consciousness is transformed.

—EUGENE TAYLOR, PH.D., Cambridge Society of the New Jerusalem
author, *William James on Consciousness beyond the Margin*

To Ted Braunud with Thanks

5 VI 07

THE HUNTER'S TRANCE

Nature, Spirit & Ecology

CARL VON ESSEN

Lindisfarne Books

2007

Lindisfarne Books

610 MAIN ST., GREAT BARRINGTON, MA 01230

WWW.LINDISFARNE.ORG

COVER IMAGE: *Hunting,* WESTERN WEI DYNASTY, 535–557 (WALL PAINTING) © MOGAO
CAVES, DUNHUANG, GANSU PROVINCE, NW CHINA / THE BRIDGEMAN ART LIBRARY
NATIONALITY / COPYRIGHT STATUS: OUT OF COPYRIGHT
COVER AND BOOK DESIGN: WILLIAM JENS JENSEN

LINES FROM "GO FISHING" BY TED HUGHES USED BY PERMISSION
IMAGES USED BY PERMISSION

 Printed on Recycled Paper

LIBRARY OF CONGRESS CATALOGING-IN-PUBLICATION DATA

von Essen, Carl, 1926–
  The hunter's trance : Nature, Spirit & Ecology / by
Carl François von Essen.
    p. cm.
  Includes bibliographical references.
  ISBN-13: 978-1-58420-045-1
  1. Nature—Religious aspects. I. Title.
  BL65.N35E87 2007
  201'.77—dc22

                                        2007001957

CONTENTS

ACKNOWLEDGEMENTS

I T ALL BEGAN in my childhood when I saw the wonder of the life in streams and tidal pools, the magnificence of mountains and giant trees and starry skies. Later there came primal quests of camping, trekking, hunting, and fishing. These adventures of spirit and body etched everlasting memories, and I came to feel a kinship with life on this small Earth and with the cosmos. I discovered that many of these feelings were shared by fellow hunters, anglers, and mountaineers. But, over the years, disturbing revelations intensified that things were not going well with humanity's connection to mother nature. My concern grew as I heard other voices, and saw in my worldwide travels increasing evidence of our destructive impact upon the wild.

A vision evolved that our spiritual bond with the natural world can be a potent path of action toward environmental healing. That vision, undoubtedly shared by many, has taken shape in this book. But in order to better understand nature spirituality (or mysticism), I, as physician and scientist, feel that it is also worthwhile to explore some of the roads and byways of mystical experience as they relate to our evolutionary, biological, and psychological connections with nature.

Without the comments and suggestions of stern critics and generous supporters alike, this project would have faltered much more often than it did. Among the initial readers were Stephen Alter, Steve Bodio, Anthony Stevens, Eugene Taylor and Edward O. Wilson, who provided authoritative comments that stoked my fire of determination to proceed.

At various stages, others, friends and colleagues, read part or all of the evolving manuscript and gave the critical leavening to this diverse and diffuse topic. They comprise, in no particular order, Joan and Herman Suit, the late Bruce Wallace, David Oswald, André Toth, Sister Elaine Prevallet, David Englund, Subhas Roy, Göran Olbers, Isabel Tellez, Mary Robson, Bishopriyo Sanyal, Nancy Wilson, Peggy and Paul Eriksson, Nicholas Helburn, the late Joe Wray, and Bill Ventigmilia. The reference librarians at the Lamont Library, Colleen Bryant, Sue Gilroy, and Julie Revak, and, at the Cambridge Public Library, Shushie Pahigian, helped me with much of the literary research. Sarah Gallogly and William Jens Jensen worked diligently to create a readable book. Gene Gollogly and Christopher Bamford gave much support and encouragement. Finally, my wife, Manisha Roy, was a beacon of inspiration to my efforts. I am deeply thankful for their input.

To the memory of Eric, 1954–1997

I walked into the forest, struck as always by the coolness of the shade beneath the tropical vegetation, and continued until I came to a small glade that opened onto the sandy path. I narrowed the world down to a few meters. Again I tried to compose the mental set—call it the naturalist's trance, the hunter's trance—by which biologists locate more elusive organisms....The effect was strangely calming. Breathing and heartbeat diminished, concentration intensified. It seemed to me that something extraordinary in the forest was very close to where I stood, moving to the surface and to discovery.

E. O. Wilson, Biophilia

The love of nature is a love of something ineffable. It is the first step on the path to mystical experience.

Graham Dunstan Martin
Shadows in the Cave

Introduction

EARLY IN HIS lifelong career as a nature photographer, Ansel Adams came to love the beauty and majesty of the California High Sierra. This is what he experienced in the summer of 1923, trekking through the rugged country east of Yosemite:

> I was climbing the long ridge west of Mount Clark. It was one of those mornings when the sunlight is burnished with a keen wind and long feathers of cloud move in a lofty sky. The silver light turned every blade of grass and every particle of sand into luminous metallic splendor; there was nothing, however small, that did not clash in the bright wind, that did not send arrows of light through the glassy air. I was suddenly arrested in the long crunching path up the ridge by an exceedingly pointed awareness of the *light*. The moment I paused, the full impact of the mood was upon me; I saw more clearly than I have ever seen before or since the minute detail of the grasses, the clusters of sand shifting in the wind, the small flotsam of the forest, the motion of the high clouds streaming above the peaks. There are no words to convey the moods of those moments....
>
> I dreamed that for a moment time stood quietly, and the vision of this actuality became but the shadow of an infinitely greater world, that I had within the grasp of consciousness a transcendental experience.[1]

What has happened? One minute the young photographer is trudging along a mountain ridge; the next, time stands still, light becomes extraordinary, every detail stands out as if etched, a memory is imprinted, and something is changed forever. Such a magical moment is surely charged with spiritual energy. Ansel Adams described his experience as transcendental, from the Latin *transcendere*, meaning to climb across or beyond, to surpass the range or grasp of human experience, reason, or belief. The biologist E. O. Wilson, too—quoted in the epigraph to this volume—felt "something extraordinary" happening in the dark glade of the jungle of Surinam as he entered the trancelike state of the stalking naturalist or hunter. It was a sense of mystery—a word whose root, *mystes*, also gave us the word "mysticism" and in ancient times signified initiation into secret rites.

To many, such experiences arising from the nurturing splendor of our natural world give depth and meaning beyond a mundane existence increasingly beset by "civilization's" superficial and materialistic values. They can burrow deep into the soul and become a conduit to an expansion of our worldview, a clearer understanding of self and of our natural world. Let us explore this dimension of experience and discover some of its surprising and varied manifestations, a part of our spiritual relationship with the natural world.

The word *mysticism* today is often cloaked in connotations of spiritualism, occultism, obscure religious sectarianism, and fuzzy thinking. Another expression, "ecstasy," from the Greek *ek* + *statikos*, meaning a displacement, to stand apart from oneself, is now so misused that, to many people, it chiefly signifies the notorious drug of the same name. Perhaps that is why writers who describe such states nowadays tend to avoid these words, replacing them with *epiphany, bliss, rapture, flow,* and *peak experience.* But I believe that the words *mysticism* and *ecstasy* deserve to be reconsidered with respect to their archaic roots, and to have their older meanings restored.

How rare are these soaring, ecstatic moments such as the one Ansel Adams experienced? It appears from several studies that many of us have experienced them. Fifteen hundred Americans in one survey by the *New York Times* were asked, "Have you ever had the feeling of being very close to a powerful spiritual force that seemed to lift you out of yourself?" About forty percent of the respondents answered, "Yes." Yet nearly all said they had never spoken about that feeling to anyone.

When I talk to fellow outdoors people—hunters, anglers, and mountaineers—about such experiences, most of them nod, often with a glint of fond recollection in their eyes, a far-off gaze recalling some indelible memory. But they do not generally volunteer to describe those moments. When the respondents in the *New York Times* survey were asked why they hadn't discussed their experience with others, the common answer was, "It didn't seem to be the kind of thing people talk about."[2] These very intimate feelings coming from the impact of a powerful spiritual encounter have also surprised me, and have been difficult to describe even to myself, let alone to others. Far removed from daily experience, they defy rational explanation. How can one share them in everyday conversation? It is like baring the soul. Indeed, we often share, as Coleridge wrote, "a cowardice of all deep feelings."[3]

Yet volumes upon volumes have been written in the attempt to capture mystical experiences—including, of course, this book. Somehow the glory of these experiences generates an urge to overcome our initial reticence and share that ecstasy with others.

Teresa of Avila, St. John of the Cross, and others had fervent ecstasies. How do such moments come to ordinary human beings? Do we have an inner site that can be lit by the transcendent spark of mystery, of a presence or power that has been given many names, but that we know only tacitly, inside ourselves?

Somewhere in the soul exists a burning light that flares up at moments of turmoil, unease, or introspection. It is an inborn need to go beyond mundane experience, beyond eating, sleeping, and procreating, to find some "ultimate truth" that can give a deeper meaning to life. It is a search for something more than what we are, a need for an ultimate relationship, beyond family, clan, and community, with a divine presence.[4] It is a thirst for transcendence, the over-belief, where mysticism and religion and transcendentalism and all other names for the deep well of our soul-search come together. It is, simply, spirituality, the vital and animating essence of a person (from the Latin spirare, to breathe). Spirituality is the manifestation of over-beliefs that transcend "the further limits of our being" and brings us into another dimension.

There are those who may not know or accept the concept of mystical experience. But I have felt something that leaves me awed and speechless, knowing that some great power has touched my life. It is a sense of vastness, of a unity with an ultimate reality. As will be seen, this numinous state, extending through a spectrum of intensity, can be associated also with sublime creativity and physical achievement and lead to unforgettable memories, to the creation of a work of art, a mathematical theorem, great athletic achievement, an architectural concept, or a complete change of one's life.

The subject of mystical experience has engaged scientists back to the origins of experimental psychology in the nineteenth century. Several have placed it into a basket of conditions often called "altered states of consciousness." These include hypnotic states; hallucinations; and out-of-body, near-death, alien abduction, and crop circle cult experiences, among other phenomena. Such "altered," "anomalous," "dissociative," or "exceptional" states of human experience have been parsed in numerous ways, classified as pathological, non-pathological, introvertive, extravertive, normal, or paranormal.[5] But I (and many others) believe that spontaneous spiritual encounters in nature are normal and healthy, wondrous gifts that arise out of the consciousness of ordinary individuals.

Some modern psychologists and others have created terms such as "peak experience," "flow," and "relaxation response" for the moments that often appear related to the exalted and spiritual encounters that may be called mystical. From athletes and others come the "groove," the "high," the "rush," the "zone," and so on. Yet when it comes to neurological studies, mystical experience seems relegated to the fringes of science—perhaps because it lies at the fringes of our consciousness, an area that still challenges the powers of investigative psychology and neurobiology. Neuroscientists seem to have great difficulty or reluctance in dealing with this area of human consciousness. In fact, a most respected scientist, Christof Koch, in his definitive work *The Quest for Consciousness*, bypasses altered states of consciousness by stating, "A comprehensive theory of consciousness will ultimately have to account for these unusual phenomena"[6]—a theory he is unable to provide. Indeed, it may be that with all our burgeoning scientific knowledge of what makes living beings tick, and of the origins and evolution of the universe and of life, our spirit will ultimately remain a mystery.

From the perspective of my own spiritual experiences and world encounters, and with an intellectual training spanning science and the humanities, I explore in this book the relationship of nature mysticism to our evolutionary connection with all living things, with the physical environment of our Earth and the universe. The opening to inner perceptions can lead to the extraordinary mystical feelings that William James described as a "vast expansion" of our ordinary waking consciousness. How does our spiritual relationship to nature translate into the need to preserve our environment?

My calling as a physician for over half a century has brought me to places where the wild once reigned but has been trampled down by the foot of humanity, by the relentless pressure of population increase and the seemingly unstoppable pollution of the biosphere. Nature has all but disappeared where large concentrations of people live, surely eroding the population's innate spiritual connection with its primeval roots. But we will see that we have an innate emotional affiliation with the natural world that has sometimes been called biophilia, a part of our nature that may be smothered by urban dust, yet can be reawakened, particularly in the younger years. And that quality may one day prove to be the key to humanity's survival on this endangered planet.

Mystical experience of nature is of particular relevance to our troubled age, bringing deeper into our consciousness and emotions the logic that nature sustains humanity as humanity must, in turn, sustain nature. But it also grants a spiritual connection to nature that goes beyond rationality, inspiring an emotional commitment that is the yin complementing the yang of intellectual understanding.

Scientists and others, such as the participants in the *New York Times* study mentioned above, seem to avoid emotional language when discussing our relationship to the environment. It is embarrassment, perhaps, a personal shyness about baring deep feelings. The naturalist David Orr points out that the word *love* is absent from the environmental literature. Perhaps, as Abraham Maslow suggested, the denial of emotions is a defense against being overwhelmed by emotions that can include humility, reverence, mystery, wonder, and awe. Yet it is likely that many individuals choose careers in biology and ecology after being moved by "an early, deep and vivid resonance between the natural world and us."[7]

I have written this book in the belief that this resonance, and the emotional commitment it engenders to all life, can similarly move the people of the world to nurture and protect this Earth as they would a loved one, to turn the tide away from destruction and toward the preservation of the biosphere on which our own survival depends. I do not claim to be able to address all the problems and possible solutions to the increasing environmental crisis. The shelves of libraries and bookshops groan from the weight of books dealing with these questions. But I aim to show how our spiritual relationship with nature must be nurtured and revived in order to bring us back, literally, to our senses, so that we can preserve what is now being destroyed.

As I have traveled the world, often on medical duties, I have witnessed the damage done around the globe by burgeoning population, violence, urban sprawl, and disease; and my memories affect me profoundly. Yet I have another set of memories, of time spent in the outdoors, ranging from the mundane to the ecstatic, that comforts me today. I have felt a need for these two worlds of my memories to somehow join in a healing process. Now, like W. H. Hudson in his bedsit in London, writing his memories and novels of Patagonia, I sit in my Cambridge apartment to write of memories but also of the mystery that can give such profound ecstatic experiences to others and myself in nature's realm. The nature mysticism that I espouse in these pages is a state of mind, a calm and contemplative way of looking at our relationship with nature, not in the vertical transcendence to a remote and greater Being but in a horizontal vision, seeing ourselves as part of this thin and fragile biosphere, our source of life and our spiritual home.

I. The Explorer

HIMALAYAN EPIPHANY

Each step I took was an effort, even though the walking was much easier now. Just beyond the amphitheater I came to a saddle in the ridge, where I collapsed beneath a moru oak.... For ten or fifteen minutes I lay there with my eyes closed and if anyone had come upon me they would have thought that I was dead.

When I eventually opened my eyes, I felt sure that I had breathed my last and gone straight to heaven. Two rays of sunlight were streaming through the branches of the oaks and falling away directly on a smaller tree that stood twenty feet away. Though it had no leaves this tree was covered in flowers that seemed to glow in the shafts of light.

Lying there against the roots of the massive oak, my first impression was that I was hallucinating, for the vision of this flowering tree and the sunlit glade were magical. I dared not move for fear of disturbing the perfection of that scene.... But in the stillness of the glade I was acutely aware of something greater than myself. Awe is the only word that might describe the experience. I had walked right past the flowering trees but in my exhaustion I hadn't noticed the blossoms and only now was I aware of their transcendent beauty. The catharsis that it evoked was so powerful that I felt weightless, as if the ground had dropped a way beneath me. Lying there, I found myself in tears, emotions welling up inside of my chest, as if the roots of the tree had penetrated deep into my soul.[8]

STEPHEN ALTER WROTE this after trekking through the foothills of the Himalayas, seeking the inner and outer sources of the religious roots and the spiritual sanctuaries of the most sacred sites of Hindu religion. Surely the sacred groves of the headwaters of the Ganges must have given the same epiphany to the first pilgrim, centuries ago, as Alter experienced on this remote ridge between the Yamuna and Bagirathi rivers. As the English geographer Paul Devereux suggests, such *loci consecrati* are recognized by a universal instinct, a part of *topophilia,* the love of place, and are associated with a mysterious power that evokes a spiritual feeling of connection.[9]

INNER EXPLORATION

Such intimate contact with nature stirs our primal self. Feelings, often buried under tons of civilization, are wrenched to the surface in a few moments. It is as if an electrical potential between the self and nature is released and a current flows that ignites a momentary ecstasy. The reality of that moment is utterly true; nothing can alter that knowing, which remains in the psyche forever. Many lovers of nature and the outdoors know this feeling. It comes often with the motion and exertion of the body that seems to condition the mind to be receptive to that magic flash of current that signifies mystical experience.

Indeed, a degree of physical stress can be the significant factor leading to the unifying feeling that total immersion in nature brings. The nature writer and Zen disciple Peter Matthiessen, for example, was caught in a terrifying storm. He became physically and emotionally overwhelmed with utter exhaustion and loss of sense of self. Finally, after the storm passed, "In the clearness of the Himalayan air, mountains draw near, and in such splendor, tears come quietly to my eyes and cool on my sunburned cheeks.... this feeling is astonishing: not so long ago I could say truthfully that I had not shed a tear in twenty years."[10] Now, unforgettably, he had felt the "heart beat of the world."

The power of nature can break through our emotional barriers. Sitting by the ocean and feeling the powerful, repetitive rhythm of the breaking waves, the physicist Fritjof Capra experienced an ecstasy so overwhelming that he burst into tears. That moment was a catharsis leading to a creative vision, *The Tao of Physics*.

Tears may often surprise the most rugged voyager, as they did Nietzsche when, trekking the hills of Italy, he felt "a rapture whose tremendous tension occasionally discharges itself in a flood of tears."[11] Who has not experienced something similar? Possibly a lump in the throat or a sob when hearing beautiful music, seeing a dramatic painting or sunset, or reading a poem. Physical exertion and the majesty of nature can combine in a chemical and psychic reaction to reach such ecstatic feelings.

Yet a quiet walk through a forest, too, can evoke deep emotion, as in Turgenev's book, *A Hunter's Sketches:* "The heart at one time throbs and beats, plunging passionately forward; at another it is drowned beyond recall in memories. Your whole life, as it were, unrolls lightly and rapidly before you; a man at such times possesses all his past, all his feelings and his powers—all his soul."[12] Turgenev had entered an inner dimension, a spiritual continuum with the natural world.

In ancient times and still in contemporary aboriginal cultures there are rituals of solitary pilgrimages into the wilderness, of vision quests supported by communal prayer and fasting, often the rites of passage to adulthood. These traditions are followed by numerous organizations and wilderness guides that bring the spiritual immanence of nature to young people.[13] One of the final tests for participants in the international program Outward Bound is to stay entirely alone in the wild for a night or more. Although I am sure the exercise is designed to further equip the participant with skills of surviving in the wilderness, it may also offer the chance to develop nature spirituality.

Mystics, religious and other, often practice longer periods of solitude and fasting, such as Jesus's forty days in the desert. The ascetic is truly emptied, psychically and physically. Neurophysiological processes, as we shall see in chapter 6, interact with the mystic's psychic emptying to allow the inner Self, the "uncluttered Throne room of God" as Barbara Brown Taylor calls it, to reverberate in harmony with the cosmos, unhampered by extraneous resistance. Jesus surely emerged from his retreat a changed man, blessed by extraordinary enlightenment. He went on to deliver the glorious humanitarian teachings that are eternal.

This sort of conditioning, in a much more modest form, through "camping out," is an experience that most of humanity in increasingly urbanized societies lacks. As the New England naturalist Henry Beston suggests, when we stray far from nature our lifeblood thins and we become spiritual wraiths. The simple experience of gazing with unfettered vision into the starry sky can renew our innate mystical connection with nature, the billions of points of light reaching deep into our souls—but such skies cannot be seen near city lights.

TOPOPHILIA

Part of our connection to nature is the feeling for a place where we belong, perhaps where we were born or had an extraordinary experience. There is a term in Swedish for this, "the place of the wild strawberries" (smultronstället), which is a secret site for which we yearn, the sacred place that will nurture and heal the spirit. From the earliest times, it is likely that this affinity for certain sites led prehistoric peoples to erect shrines and temples where they could feel the heartbeat of the Earth. These were surely the roots of organized religions. Often they were places with particular unions of water, trees, and mountains. Humankind seeks such places even at great distances. Such are the great holy shrines of India at the headwaters of the Ganges that Stephen Alter saw and wrote about.

For many years I have returned regularly to a secret "place of the wild strawberries" in northern New Mexico. I will forever remember that day of discovery when wading up a small river high in the Jemez

Mountains. My slow exploration of the San Antonio had led up past the gorge to a bend in the river around which I saw a spectacular sight: the towering brick red cliffs of the outer edge of the ancient crater loomed above; beyond, the canyon suddenly widened, bisected by the now peacefully meandering stream bordered by alpine meadows. At the bend, one meadow was encircled by willows, aspens, and firs to form a small natural amphitheater. From this meadow I could look upstream to see the red cliffs now glowing like fire from the light of the setting sun. Above was the translucent dark blue through which pierced the distant cold light of Venus. The beauty and harmony of the setting transmitted equanimity straight into my soul.[14]

That place tugged at me to return again and again to feel a mysterious nurturing of my spirit as I camped for days, alone except for the occasional beaver and bear, and left refreshed.[15] Why do certain places evoke the feelings that I had? Those with a Freudian bent may postulate that it represents a desire to return to the comfort of the womb. Perhaps so, but it is the womb of creation, of our Mother Nature. These deep and primal connections led Paul Devereux to write, in *The Sacred Place,* "The idea of the holy was inherent in the landscape from all time and it was the landscape that made it stir within our heart and mind."[16]

Children, their innate spirituality still unhampered by the burdens of materialism, often instinctively seek solitary sites that offer beauty and peace. Secret gardens and murmuring brooks are places of refuge that can give the opportunity for imaginative journeys. These "ecstatic places," according to the child psychologist Louise Chawla, evoke "ecstatic memories (that) shine like jewels within the casing of our lives."[17]

Water is often a special attraction in our search for pleasure and comfort. It is our ultimate original mother, the nurturing medium of the origins of life. I experience a mysterious yearning particularly for salt water. Without the occasional swim, most months of the year, I feel a certain emptiness. Water sports and joyous splashings in rivers, ponds, waterfalls, and ocean surf form the matrix of fond memories of childhood and youth. It is sad to realize that so many people, often raised in urban settings, have scarcely ever splashed freely in natural bodies of water and may even be unable to swim. Beings raised in nature near an aquatic setting take to water as part of the total environmental experience.

At the very beginning of the American classic *Moby Dick,* Herman Melville, through his protagonist Ishmael, captures the power that attracts us to this element, a part of the immense fabric of nature. Ishmael observes the New Yorkers "pent up in lath and plaster—tied to couches, nailed to benches, cinched to desks," flocking to the waterfronts and seashores on Sundays, "fixed in ocean reveries."[18] Ishmael's fellow citizens are attracted like the magnetized needle of a compass to the water. Truly, as he says, meditation and water are wedded together. The sound of the waves, the murmur of the brook, the crash of a waterfall give us connections to all that we have been and all that we will be.

For individuals with no knowledge of nature, an intense experience of the wilderness may change forever their relationship to the Earth mother. As we have seen again and again, our deepest emotions are grounded in transcendent moments that sweep through consciousness, revealing a vast dimension of reality of which we are ordinarily not aware. The veils of preconceived and acquired notions of beauty and order may suddenly drop, revealing a breathtaking inner or outer vision. It may be like seeing a familiar thing truly for the first time. This essence of a mystical moment is transformative, indelible, and true. The merging of elements from a transcendent moment in a natural setting nurtures unforgettable memories of the ecstatic places, the places of wild strawberries, the spirit of place.

The evocation of the senses through such memories may lead to further transcendental experiences. In the classic example, Marcel Proust through his protagonist felt "an exquisite pleasure" upon tasting a petite madeleine, an "all-powerful joy" that gave a feeling of detachment and freedom from mediocrity and mortality. That ecstasy erupted from remote, dormant memories of childhood pleasure and comfort and ranged beyond pleasure into a new dimension, an ineffable feeling that Proust eagerly sought to retrieve.

The evocation of distant memories of place, of the wild—the sound of a waterfall or the ocean beach, the smell of the pine forest, the sight of the billowing colors of a sunset—all can trigger similar ecstasies. Are these memories of one's own experience of the senses or are they from ancient origins? Proust hinted at deeper sources:

> But when from a long distant past nothing subsists, after the people are dead, after the things are broken and scattered, taste and smell alone, more fragile but more enduring, more immaterial, more persistent, more faithful, remain poised a long time, like souls, remembering, awaiting, hoping, amid the ruins of all the rest; and bear unflinchingly, in the tiny drop of their essence, the vast structure of recollection.[19]

That long-distant past may include deeply hidden evolutionary roots of our inherent attachment to nature. Our Earth is home, and its natural settings evoke emotional responses that geographer Yi-Fu Tuan discusses in his book *Topophilia,* including the seashore, the valley, and the island.[20] Mountains, too, evoke the awe often encountered in great cathedrals, the reciprocally inverted spaces that also foster the conditions for mystical experience. I recall, with a frisson of awe, the sight of the great eighth-century Kailasa Temple near Ellora in central India. It is magnificently carved from the solid rock cliffs in a shape evoking the Himalayan peak Kailas, sacred to all Hindus and itself the physical embodiment of the mythical Mount Meru, the Cosmic Mountain. The temple emits a vibration, an aura of spirit, a genus loci, that conveys a sense of timeless mystery; its silence is charged with a profound presence, E. M. Forster's description in *A Passage to India* of the deep and resonant boum inside the Marabar cave.

Topophilia and biophilia may have common roots, neural connections called engrams that developed over millions of years.[21] This "environmental sensibility" is what Paul Shepard believes can lead to the ecological and sociological connections with people and the natural world, and may be most powerful when bonding with nature occurs in childhood.[22]

THE DESPOTIC EYE AND GOETHE'S PHANTASIE

> I speak in recollection of a time
> When the bodily eye, in every stage of life
> The most despotic of our senses, gained
> Such strength in 'me' as often held my mind
> In absolute dominion. Gladly here,
> Entering upon abstruser argument,
> Could I unfold the means
> Which Nature studiously employs to thwart
> This tyranny, summons all the senses each
> To counteract the other, and themselves,
> And makes them all, and the objects with which all
> Are conversant, subservient in their turn
> To the great ends of Liberty and Power.
>   WORDSWORTH, *The Prelude*, Book Twelfth

> An object, if it were before
> My eye, was by Dame Nature's law,
> Within my soul.
>   THOMAS TRAHERNE, "My Spirit"

> Man must look at nature with a supernatural eye.
>   RALPH WALDO EMERSON, "Method of Nature"

Visions of mountains, seas, rivers, and forests can expand perceptions that lead the beholder toward a transcendent communion with nature. Spinoza considered that the universe contained creative forces comprehended only through intuition, not by mathematics. He influenced Goethe's way of looking at nature, which included what the German polymath called *exakte sinnliche Phantasie* as the pathway from the sensation of observation (*Sinne*) to the subconscious imagination (*Phantasie*).[23] The literary critic and Goethe scholar Norman Skillen comments,

> What Goethe meant by this is the practical application of imagination as an instrument of scientific observation. As such it represents a slowing down and a conscious cultivation of the "oceanic feeling." The oceanic feeling is a spontaneous expansion of consciousness through which natural phenomena acquire an unaccustomed depth, become charged with meaning, seem to lose their separateness both from each other and their observer, and appear in all their intense relatedness.[24]

"Deep Form," a term coined by the ecopsychologists Betty and Theodore Roszak, means "a correspondence between the formative processes of the mind and the formative processes in nature." Like Goethe's *exakte sinnliche Phantasie,* it represents the power of our imagination to create a connection between the observed object and something deep in our psyche. Such participatory consciousness represents to me the deep inspiration that can occur in the quiet contemplation of an ocean, a sunset, or a mountain vista.

In some memorable sentences from his first and greatest book, *Nature,* Ralph Waldo Emerson said succinctly, to the admiration of many but also the amusement of unimaginative contemporaries: "Standing on the bare ground, —my head bathed by the blithe air, and uplifted into infinite space, —all mean egotism vanishes. I become a transparent eye-ball. I am nothing. I see all"[25] (see page 17).

Emerson's words breathe a truth that, as will be seen, may expand to encompass the universe. The physicist John Archibald Wheeler created, apparently entirely independently, a similar image of Emerson's all-seeing eyeball. Wheeler's model stems from his position that our understanding of the origin of the cosmos, "the building of all that is," is dependent upon the revolutionary law of quantum mechanics. That cosmic image can scarcely be grasped through our

"Standing on the bare ground, — my head
bathed by the blithe air, & uplifted into
infinite space, — all mean egotism
vanishes. I become a transparent
Eyeball."   Nature, p. 13.

The universe through the eye of Ralph Waldo Emerson. "Standing on the bare
ground—my head bathed by the blithe air, & uplifted into infinite space,—all
mean egotism vanishes. I become a transparent Eyeball." (Emerson, Nature,
13) A caricature drawn by his friend and fellow Transcendentalist, Christopher
Pearce Cranch. Illustrations of the New Philosophy, 1835 (by permission of the
Houghton Library, Harvard University).

The universe through the eye of the physicist John Archibald Wheeler. "The universe, symbolized by the letter U, starts small at the big bang (upper left), grows in size, gives rise to life and observers, and observing equipment; and the observing equipment, in turn, through the elementary quantum processes that terminate on it, takes part in giving a tangible 'reality' to events that occurred long before there was any life anywhere." (Wheeler, in Elvee, Mind in Nature, *18) One could imagine Wheeler's observing equipment to be Emerson's transparent Eyeball that is viewing all eternity.*

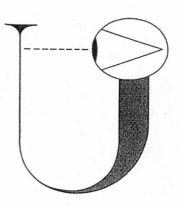

mundane intellect; it may require a truly mystical disassociation from our everyday perceptions.

Emerson, seeing all, enters the quantum world of Wheeler's eyeball that records its reciprocal connection to a universe without boundary in space or time.[26] The reality of that experience, according to Emerson, transcends all the values of what we know through our senses as the concrete and materialistic world. Wheeler's *Participatory Principle* argues that the "observer" brings reality to the universe. Without our senses there would be no universe. The all-seeing eyeball, the observer, transmits and merges the universe into the consciousness, recalling the participatory imagination of Goethe, as Emerson feels the "currents of the Universal Being circulate through me; I am part or particle of God."

When I search or stalk in a wilderness, the "despotic eye" of Wordsworth's poem becomes passive. My senses merge in quiet harmony, in an inner world where I seem to intuitively join the object and share its total being. I become like Emerson's transparent eyeball and all "mean egotism" vanishes. I stalk a trout and somehow become part of it. Its thoughts, reactions, its life history and evolution (of what I may know) flash through my mind. The stream, trees, and sky all seem to crystallize into a small universe of a new understanding of meaning. I am strangely moved—and ecstatic. I sometimes feel that my comprehension of that scene is so full that I could write an encyclopedia about it.

Direct cognitive vision probes and analyzes. I watch marvels of creation through the microscope, whirling rotifers, probing paramecia, and oozing amoebae. I stop thinking and through associative processes another vision unfolds: a vision of these animalcules in a time warp of evolution, in a creative broth containing my ancestral cell. I see not just with the eye, but also through the eye.

Helen Keller, blind and deaf, was blessed with a "spiritual vision" that enabled her to perceive, through inner recesses of her creative imagination and extraordinary senses, the energy of the living world:

> My mystic world is lovely with trees and clouds and stars and eddying streams I have never "seen." I am often conscious of beautiful flowers and birds and laughing children when to my associates there is nothing. The skeptical declare that I see "light that never was on sea or land," but I know that this mystic sense is dormant and that is why there are so many barren places in their lives.[27]

William Blake, too, believed that our physical senses limited a greater awareness, for in *The Marriage of Heaven and Hell* he reminded us of "An immense world of delight, clos'd by your senses five."

There can be two landscapes—one outside the self, the other within. The external landscape comprises the details of topography, the plants and animals, weather, geology, and evolution. The second landscape is an interior projection, the speculations, intuitions, and ideas relating to the exterior with purpose and order.[28] This evocative mindscape is a transcendental correspondence perceived through Emerson's all-seeing eyeball.

Thoreau coined in his journal an apt expression of this perceptive process: "a sauntering of the eye."[29] He derives this term, no doubt, from Wordsworth's "relaxed attention," which he quotes earlier in the journal. The seeing begins when understanding ceases; that is, the cognitive process may hinder the attainment of pure vision.

The keen powers of observation that Thoreau used to write his detailed descriptions developed with years of practice. Eventually this disciplined method evolved into a deeper, less conscious process whereby vision expanded into a new dimension of an "utter, non-controlling openness to the perceptible universe."[30] It is reasonable to speculate that the opening of the channels of perception into deeper recesses of consciousness can lead to enhanced interactions with memory and association. The sensations that flow through those channels are not merely passive; they ultimately help to create, somewhere deep in our psyche, our own worldview.

This extension of visual perception into the imaginative dimensions of the mind is linked by the art theorist Jonathan Crary to esthetics and scientific knowledge.[31] The powerful connection between imaginative perception and the spiritual feelings that arises from contact with nature, "Platonic sight," was perhaps the inspiration for Goethe in developing his theories of color and of participatory sensation. Thoreau, too, described the colors of a sunset, but in an extraordinary and wonderful way:

> I witness a beauty in the form or coloring of the clouds which addresses itself to my imagination, for which you account scientifically to my understanding, but do not so account to my imagination.... I, standing twenty miles off, see a crimson cloud in the horizon. You tell me it is a mass of vapor which absorbs all other rays and reflects the red, but that is nothing to the purpose, for this red vision excites me, stirs my blood, and I have new and indescribable fancies, and you have not touched the secret of that influence. If there is not something mystical in your explanation, something unexplainable to the understanding, some elements of mystery, it is quite insufficient. If there is nothing in it which speaks to the imagination, what boots it? What sort of science is that which enriches the understanding, but robs the imagination?[32]

That passionate statement and question ring true with my own feelings upon seeing a winter sunset in a similar New England sky. Thoreau wrote that the "least film of thought" from such a sensory experience could lead, stepwise through building and comparing of different concepts, to developing truths that are practical for everyday life. The power of imaginative association is the essence of Thoreau's statement and a basic tenet of Goethe's science.

In his controversial theory of color Goethe addressed the ineffable, the unexplainable, emotional dimension of a vision like Thoreau's. Indeed, we know that color, as we perceive it, does not exist in the material universe. As the Swiss chemist Albert Hofmann, the discoverer of LSD, reminds us, "The optical range of what we call reality does not exist on the outside; it exists on the psychic screen inside every individual."[33]

Only our five senses provide the conduit of information from the outer world to our consciousness. The opening to the inner perceptions that can lead to the extraordinary mystical feelings that have been described is a "vast expansion," as William James put it, of our ordinary waking consciousness. It is a transmission into the recesses of the spirit, of a noetic reality. Swedenborg asserted that a person has two forms of sight, one from cognitive faith, and the other from love. Cognitive vision has a correspondence with this internal sight, "the light above that of the world."[34]

Many who have described mystical experiences, particularly in nature, repeatedly remark upon "seeing things more clearly than ever seen before," of "seeing something as it truly was." Such experiences can come to us through the other senses as well. I once heard David Harrington, a member of the Kronos Quartet, describe the playing of a single note: "That note—what I feel is the essence—I have experienced maybe three or four times in my career. It is that essence that we all seek."[35]

The Native American Lakotas believe that the physical world is a spirit seen from without and that the spiritual world is the physical viewed from another dimension. The vision quest is a journey, according

to the anthropologist Elaine Jahner, to an inner spiritual landscape
that points the way through the physical landscape. The quester may
experience a moment when sensations intensify and something sacred
is revealed, leading him or her to another realm of reality. Jahner
describes this experience from the vision quest of this hunting tribe:

> The vision (generally a dream) gave its seeker the courage
> to face the mysterious dimensions of life with the calm
> foreknowledge that comes from a personal sense of mystery
> and an inner departure for the continuing journey of
> exploration that is life itself. The light of the vision illumines
> some of the night of uncertainty for both the individual and
> the group. Or, to use another set of images, the vision is a way
> of climbing a hill so high that the visionary has a perspective
> from which to view the many lower hills stretching toward
> the horizon of death.[36]

This way of thinking has also been described by the American philosopher Charles Saunders Peirce, who said that "mind is matter seen
from the inside, and matter is mind seen from the outside."[37]

I had the following experience while fishing in Patagonia. The
Rio Petrohué was swift and the wading treacherous. René, my guide,
carefully led me across, hand in hand. Our verbal communication
was in a few words of English or Spanish but much more was non-
verbal: gestures, looks, what is now often called "body language."
René was Mapuché, native to this part of Chilean Patagonia. Spanish was his second language and English a very distant third. He
was perhaps five feet four inches tall, with a powerful, stocky body,
broad face, and warm, sparkling, grave Mongolian eyes. We had been
together three days now, and I had observed him closely. His senses
were superbly acute, fine-tuned to the surroundings. He saw a hawk,
a rare plant, and a deep dwelling fish far earlier than I, oblivious to so
much that he saw, smelled, or simply, inexplicably, sensed.

He pointed to where a large trout lurked under a bank. I did not
see it. I tried to cast the big fly to that spot clear across the stream.

The fly failed to reach its target. I had tried too hard. Finally he took my rod, cast rapidly and accurately to the far shore, and retrieved the line in short jerks. A dark shadow seemed to follow, the water surface convulsed, and René shouted, "¡Hola, trucha!" Rene's natural and fluid movements spoke volumes about our differences. After releasing the big Rainbow we shook hands and lay down to rest on the grassy bank. René smiled and said, "Next time."

SOLITUDE

Solitude is a nearly universal precondition for mystical experience in nature. Emerson writes,

> To go into solitude, a man needs to retire as much from his chamber as from society. I am not solitary whilst I read and write, though nobody is with me. But if a man would be alone, let him look at the stars. The rays that come from those heavenly worlds will separate between him and what he touches. One might think the atmosphere was made transparent with this design, to give man, in the heavenly bodies, the perpetual presence of the sublime.[38]

Solitude nurtures our deepest thoughts and feelings. While these thoughts can occur anywhere—in a study, a monk's cell, or a crowded airport—the space that nature provides is an unsurpassed vessel of generosity and receptivity. My memories of nights at sea or camping in the mountains are filled with the brilliance of the universe, the stars and galaxies throbbing in luminous energy, a direct beacon for the unitive experience that is termed "mystical." My ego is humbled and tempers my thoughts and questions about the purpose of life.

The capacity to be alone is a form of self-reliance. Solitude provides the quiet space that is needed for contemplation, prayer, and originality of thought. It gives the opportunity to get in touch with our deepest feelings and to reassess them in respect to the ever-changing conditions of the outer world. Most of the mystical experiences that are described in this book occurred in solitude. In *Solitude: A Return to the Self*, the English psychiatrist Anthony Storr writes,

> some development of the capacity to be alone is necessary if the brain is to function at its best, and if the individual is to fulfill his highest potential. Human beings easily become alienated from their deepest needs and feelings. Learning, thinking, innovation, and maintaining contact with one's own inner world are all facilitated by solitude.[39]

Storr equates many experiences of solitude, voluntary or involuntary (such as when imprisoned) with moments of ecstasy. As Richard Byrd poetically expressed it in describing winter in the Antarctic, one comes away "humbled with the beauty and the miracle of aloneness."[40]

With solitude comes simplicity. Anne Morrow Lindbergh reflects on the simple bare beauty of a channeled whelk shell found on the beach. She compares it to the shape of her life: "How untidy it has become! Blurred with moss, knobby with barnacles, it's hardly recognizable anymore." She seeks "a singleness of eye, a purity of intention, a central core of my life" in order to live in inner harmony, "in grace." In this pursuit she adopts a practice of simplicity, living alone on the beach, shedding clothes, furniture, and the chattel that accumulates like moss around our lives. "How little one (can) get along with," she exclaims, "and what extraordinary freedom and peace such simplification can bring."[41]

Her words resonate in me as I contemplate the frenetic pace of urban life, increasing throughout the world along with the capacity of IT (information technology) to direct our easily manipulated minds. Solitude for many with few inner resources, according to one psychologist, may lead to depression, passivity, and other "negative states."[42] Viewing the London scene of over two hundred years ago, Wordsworth deplored the craving for "extraordinary moment" and for "outrageous stimulation." Our modern culture, too, tends to replace the spaces of our inner resources with psychic noise: sensational entertainment, gadgets, toys, and other basically unnecessary paraphernalia.

Certainly we seek and need interaction with fellow human beings, but it seems that the self-reliance of which Emerson spoke so eloquently is disappearing in many evolving materialistic cultures, East and West.

SPIRIT IN NATURE

> Several of nature's people
> I know, and they know me;
> I feel for them a transport
> Of cordiality.
>
> EMILY DICKINSON

My thoughts return continually to the words of the nature mystic Henry David Thoreau. The essay "Walking" expresses the kernel of his philosophy that is so close to my heart: "I believe that there is a subtle magnetism in Nature, which, if we subconsciously yield to it, will direct us aright."[43] Thoreau's words soar as he recalls the joys of walking in New England: "So we saunter toward the Holy Land, till one day the sun shall shine more brightly than ever he has done, shall perchance shine into our minds and hearts, and light up our lives with a great awakening light, as warm and serene and golden as on a bankside in autumn."[44]

Thoreau saw Walden Pond in a creative dimension that unified him with the object of his vision and daily sensibility. His perception of the wind moving over water recalls images we now have of the dynamic whorls of cloud seen from space. He surely felt the living unity now called Gaia when he wrote:

> A field of water betrays the spirit that is in the air. It is continually receiving new life and motion from above. It is intermediate in its nature between land and sky. On land only the grass and trees wave, but the water itself is rippled by the wind. I see where the breeze dashes across it by the streaks or flakes of light. It is remarkable that we can look down on its surface. We shall,

perhaps, look down thus on the surface of air at length, and mark where a subtler spirit sweeps over it.[45]

Unlike the mystical transports, no longer experienced, that remain fond and unforgettable memories, this harmonic resonance with the elemental natural forces persists in me even into old age. Those forces have been described sometimes as moody, unforgiving, or vengeful. But nature's "terror" is alien to the Taoist who considers the natural world to be a spiritual home. Nature is impassive: it just—is. No anthropocentrism is called for. I feel at home in the face of storms as well as sunsets.

The correspondence between the outer world, nature, and our inner world, spirit, brought Emerson to wonder about "the secret sympathy that connects man to all animals and all the inanimate beings around him." In fact, he said, "The whole of nature is a metaphor of the human mind."[46] This cornerstone of New England transcendentalism furthered the belief in the common origins of all life and, indeed, all reality. Thus the individual Self merged with nature in a harmonious unity. As I walk in the woodlands around Walden Pond a shiver of revelation often comes as I feel the shades of Emerson, Alcott, Thoreau, and other Concord friends wandering the same paths, feeling the same emotions of the glorious conjunction with fellow-life. The feeling of the immanence of God could have been the purest joy of those quiet walks from Concord.

This affinity or vibration evokes the doctrine of *correspondences* that Emmanuel Swedenborg, the Swedish mystic and theologian developed: "The intercourse of the soul with the body is such as is the influx of the spiritual world with the natural…this is according to correspondences."[47] Similarly, Thoreau asks, "Is it not as language that all natural objects affect the poet? He sees a flower or other object, and it is beautiful or affecting to him because it is a symbol of his thought…. The objects I behold correspond to my mood."[48]

The correspondences of Swedenborg lie at the roots of New England transcendentalism and pervade the mystical connection with nature. Eugene Taylor suggests that the psychological significance of correspondences is to express the symbolism of nature whereby spiritual truths are found in the observed objects: "Each leaf...rich in poetic memory; each twig a light toward self-knowledge"[49]

Our present knowledge of evolution and of the biosphere enhances the appreciation of Thoreau's vision, so limited in its sentience by his parochial New England, yet limitless in its spirit and his message to the modern world. Thoreau inhaled the enchantment of that time beside Walden Pond and expressed his feelings in ecstatic passages: "Sometimes we are clarified and calmed healthily as we were never before in our lives—not by an opiate—but by some subconscious obedience to the all-just laws—so that we become like a still lake of purest crystal and without effort our depths are revealed to ourselves."[50]

I visit a farm in Sweden, in an area of exceptional wildness, of lakes and forests, with few signs of human ingress. My host, bluff and hearty, from a long lineage of local peasants, knows the land and all thereon, through centuries of transmitted and inherited wisdom. Tourists, refugees from overdeveloped and overcrowded parts of continental Europe, have found this Nordic oasis of the spirit. The farmer appreciates why they hunger for nature and proposes to develop a "healing resort," not by building stark new cabins but by renovating some old abandoned cottages, widening a few paths through the dense forest, and providing boats on a few of the many lakes. The impact of his entrepreneurial ambitions upon the nature he loves will be small; perhaps the impact upon tense, harried inhabitants from concrete warrens will be great.

We see the magnetic pull of nature upon human instincts in everyday life when people flock to the seashore, mountains, and woods for "relaxation," yet what is fundamentally healing is the filling of the emptiness most of us experience in urban and semi-urban existence. The greater Mother is nature and its loss or absence can produce deep lacunae in our souls. The naturalist Sigurd Olson canoed through the vast and remote waterways of the Quetico-Superior Wilderness and felt that power when he wrote in *The Singing Wilderness.* "Uncounted centuries of the primitive have left their mark upon us, and civilization has not changed emotional needs that were ours before the dawn of history."[51]

Henry Beston gives voice to our yearning for a closer relationship with nature in *Outermost House,* the account of a sojourn in a small cabin on Cape Cod. "The world today is sick to its thin blood for lack of elemental things, for fire before the hands, for water welling from the Earth, for air, for the dear earth underfoot. In my world of beach and dune these elemental presences lived and had their being, and under their arch there moved an incomparable pageant of nature and the year."[52]

The nature writer W. H. Hudson, who was reared on the pampas of southern Argentina, expressed the impact of natural environment in our primal psyche when he wrote of "animism, or that sense of something in nature which to the enlightened or civilized man is ...but a faint survival of a phase of the primitive mind." Hudson's animism was a projection of himself into nature. He felt that there existed an intelligence more powerful than his own, inhabiting "all visible things" and most accessible to those, like himself, "born and bred amidst rural surroundings, where there are hills and woods and rocks and streams and waterfalls, these being the conditions which are most favorable to it—the scenes that have 'inherited associations' for us."[53]

Those feelings represent a superabundance of joy and enthusiasm, the knowing that we are truly connected. They are deeply etched into our memories and often bring fresh upwellings of fond emotions years and decades later. Nearing my ninth decade of life there is comfort, balance, and perspective as I recall those unforgettable moments of my past. They leaven the burden and struggle that is inevitable in human existence.

As I, far from light-bedecked Cambridge, watch the night sky high up in the Rockies, the dazzling vision of the heavens stirs a primal feeling. I wonder what the impact of that cosmic power was on the minds of our early ancestors. From the ancient megaliths that many believe to be ancient astronomical observatories, we can speculate that it guided them toward observation and measurement. But it may also have had a mystical and unitive impact, giving them the feeling of the connection of their destiny with the forces of nature.

The essence of mystic experience in nature may indeed be the apprehension that we are not apart from the world, the unitive dimension, which is the basis, as I urge, of biophilia. The exhilaration of being in nature, those treasured moments of transcendence and self-affirmation, can bring the spirit to a crystalline level of aware-ness of cosmic unity. These meditative, exaltational, and trancelike states are none other than intense moments of nearly total awareness. They are the complete opposite of the ecstatic drug scene, where "dropping out" of the world appears to be the goal. This antithesis is at the heart of opposing worldviews of our moral commitment to preserving the biosphere. I believe that the world of "recreational" drugs reflects the sickness that has infested a generation or more with cynicism and pessimism about our future.

Far from "dropping out," the expansion of consciousness binds the mystic to his surroundings in a way that so often is said to be unitive. That unitive feeling can lead to creative effort, composing a work of art, performing a surgical operation, or making love. It lies at the heart of our evolutionary bond with nature and supports our efforts for saving the biosphere and ourselves.

Beauty is nature—plants, animals, minerals, landscapes evoke emotions that are part of our evolutionary heritage. That heritage, the very development of life on Earth, is the subject of the next chapter. The aesthetic appeal of nature, the imprinting of the struc-ture of the universe upon our thoughts and our sense of beauty, is an important part of biophilia, which the social ecologist Stephen Kellert suggests was an advantage in human evolution leading to the increased likelihood of acquiring nourishment and protection.[54] If that was true for early humanity, it is even truer now, as that appre-ciation guides our spirit and our actions to protect and restore the mother that nurtured us from our very beginnings.

2. Evolution

Suddenly from behind the rim of the moon, in long, slow-motion moments of immense majesty, there emerges a sparkling blue and white jewel, a light, delicate sky-blue sphere laced with slowly swirling veils of white, rising gradually like a small pearl in a thick sea of dark majesty. It takes more than a moment to fully realize this is Earth ... home.

Edgar Mitchell, *The Home Planet*

The Earth is not a mere fragment of dead history, stratum upon stratum like the leaves of a book, but living poetry like the leaves of a tree, which precede flowers and fruit—not a fossil Earth, but a living Earth, compared with whose great central life all animal and vegetable life is merely parasitic.

Henry Thoreau, *Walden*

Chaos

A S ETERNITY IS said to be a blink of Brahma's eye, so is the span of life on Earth a fleeting iota in cosmic history—and the existence of humankind a mere hiccup in Earth's living history. As our knowledge increases, however, in sciences such as chemistry, physics, biology, paleontology, and cosmology, so does our power to seek our tiny tendrils in the origins of the universe and of life. From that ferment of new techniques and knowledge come possibilities of finding our psychic roots as well, although we have yet to find fossils of the mind.

The awareness of the vast dimension of evolutionary time and space linking humankind to its natural roots may sometimes be startling. On a journey through East Africa Carl Jung watched vast herds of wild animals grazing in "soundless stillness," as they had done from time immemorial. "I felt then as if I were the first man, the first creature to know that it is. The whole world around me was still in the primitive silence and knew not that it was. In this very moment in which I knew it the world came into existence and without this moment it would never have been."[55]

We inhabit an amazingly diverse living world. The growing knowledge of our deepest evolutionary roots can guide us, through all the strata of awareness and consciousness, to a better understanding of our place in the natural world. The philosopher Karl Popper considered that there was a "mind-like behavior" early in evolutionary history, while William James suggested that consciousness might have existed "at the very origin of things." With those thoughts in mind, I will try to briefly describe some significant events that have contributed to the evolution of our protean biosphere and to our existence.

According to some scientists, a major cosmic collision that happened about four and a half billion years ago established conditions contributing to the eventual creation of life. Our NASA program was responsible for the scientific studies leading to this dramatic story. The Apollo mission brought back lunar rocks that have now been studied for decades. From their analysis, scientists now generally agree on the theory that a gigantic asteroid, estimated to be the size of Mars, collided with the newly formed Earth. This massive cataclysm dislodged a large chunk of molten magma, perhaps from what is now the large basin containing the Pacific Ocean. This mass eventually condensed into the sphere that is now our moon. At the same time that this collision occurred, the Earth's axis may have been knocked askew. Through the billions of years of our Earth's history, the axis of rotation has been tilted about twenty-three degrees from the normal, relative to our sun. Whether this was a direct result of the gigantic collision is not clear, but we do know that the orbiting moon exerts a gravitational pull that holds the Earth's axis to that angle. If not thus stabilized, the Earth's axis would wobble as much as eighty-five degrees—too much to support life as we know it.[56]

The Earth's tilt is responsible for the seasonal changes that are so familiar to us now—and that also may have led to the conditions for the generation and evolution of the first forms of life. According to experts, the fluctuating environments of temperature, water vapor, and carbon compounds made possible the first reproductive events, then modulated the evolutionary changes that led to the present-day kaleidoscopic array of life.[57]

It was at least half a billion years after that asteroidal collision, that some forms of life emerged from the hot bubbling oceans. Eventually one organism evolved, perhaps three billion years ago (*bya*), into what is called "the Last Universal Common Ancestor." Charles Darwin, when summing up his *Origin of Species,* concluded, "probably all the organic beings which have ever lived on this Earth have descended from some one primordial form, into which life was first breathed."[58] Darwin seems to have been largely right. It is now considered probable that the source of life that led to our existence, and that of all living organisms today, was a single progenitor, a bit of protoplasm that came into existence in that chaos and possessed the remarkable ability to multiply[59] That proto-cell contained a genetic code that reproduced itself, most times exactly. We may stem, every individual organism, from the smallest bacterium to the largest tree, from the simplest to the most complex, from that single event.[60] Some of the relatively unchanged descendents of these earliest ancestral organisms still survive around the superheated thermal fumaroles under our oceans. At some point our ancestral cells developed characteristics that are today shared by all living cells: the ability to grow, reproduce, inherit, and mutate. A fifth characteristic, awareness, a quality that may lie at the very heart of the origins of what we know as consciousness, slowly evolved through the communication and organization of cells. Molecular signals transmitted between cells have led to multicellularity and coordinated behavior.[61]

We are rather lucky to exist, all because of these accidents in the chaos of early cosmic time. Some cosmologists believe that the circumstances leading to the origins of life were exceptional. In fact, they believe that the existence of other life as we know it in the universe is much less likely than has been predicted by simple probability calculations.

The intellectual recognition of our common molecular architecture enhances the emotional link that I feel with life all around me. When I gaze up at a lofty sequoia or down upon the myriads of insects at my feet there is sheer love. They are not strangers; they are part of me and I of them.

ORGANIZATION

These earliest ancestors survived by the process of fermentation of the organic molecules in the ancient ocean broth. But as the Earth cooled, over millions of years, the energy available for the metabolism of these early cells diminished. Ever multiplying, the cells consumed what little organic matter there was in that stark environment. This amounted to a population explosion, eerily akin to the crisis we humans are facing today. Our ancestors simply ran out of food.

Somehow, as their sources of energy diminished, they evolved in a way that accomplished the truly revolutionary takeover of the Earth's environment—the radical transformation of our atmosphere. The primitive protobacteria developed the ability to utilize the sun's energy to metabolize much more abundant chemicals, by-products of the fermentation reactions, such as carbon dioxide and hydrogen sulfide. These cyanobacteria (which still exist and are often, and incorrectly, referred to as blue-green algae) also metabolized the ever-present water and produced free oxygen as a waste product.

The oxygen-producing organelles of these primitive cyanobacteria became incorporated into eukaryotes, "modern" cells with distinct nuclei.[62] The bacterial nuclear material containing the all-important chemical chlorophyll was incorporated into the eukaryotes as tiny bodies called chloroplasts.

This astonishing event has led to the preservation and continuation of all life on Earth. It was now possible to use the sun's energy to metabolize water and carbon dioxide to generate oxygen and carbohydrates. That process revolutionized our biosphere through the radical transformation of the atmosphere.

Earth, following the cataclysm of its origin, gradually became enveloped by a gaseous layer of carbon dioxide, nitrogen, and water vapor, just like the stratum surrounding our neighboring planets, Mars and Venus, even to this day. By three bya, however, oxygen was being formed by photosynthetic bacteria and later chloroplast-bearing eukaryotes, gradually transforming our atmosphere. Since about 2.3 bya, Earth's atmosphere has consisted, in about the same proportions, of a mixture of nitrogen, oxygen, and carbon dioxide.[63] Life evolved to use the only plentiful energy source—solar radiation—through oxidative (oxygen-dependent) metabolism, hence most organisms today are utterly dependent on this biologically generated gas for survival.

This biological revolution demonstrates that early life was aware of its environment, developing survival skills that eventually led through a seamless evolution to our own existence. Humanity's psyche may therefore be a direct descendent of those events billions of years ago when cells struggled to adapt to their circumstances, and, through the process of adapting, transformed the biosphere.

In his *Cell and Psyche,* the biologist Edmund Sinnot proposed more than fifty years ago that biological organization and consciousness are fundamentally similar. He postulated that "The primary reason for the rise of higher types of psychological behavior, culminating in mind, seems to have been the necessity of speedy regulating reactions to insure the survival of motile organisms in a complex and changing environment."[64] That capability to communicate and thus to organize was the first step of the evolution of mind, a property that all complex organisms share, including humankind.[65] The evolutionary psychologist Howard Bloom postulates "connectionism"—perhaps another way of saying "biological organization"—as the mechanism of psychic evolution from primordial life to the present.[66]

Possibly the first sustainable organized systems of life were the cyanobacteria that created stromatolites three bya, mats of organisms seeking better living conditions and growing into various shapes that are seen today in fossilized structures. Their existence indicates that indeed awareness, cooperation, and motility were necessary parts of survival close to the very beginning of life.

Even as far back as the nineteenth century the French experimental psychologist Alfred Binet was captivated by the behavioral patterns of protozoa. He described in his book *The Psychic Life of Micro-Organisms* the complex activities of conglomerations of these cells—"pluricellular organisms"—and suggested that their purposeful actions represented a psychic transition from unicellular eukaryotes to the metazoa (the group to which all complex animal systems belong).[67]

From the fossil evidence of their archebacterial ancestors that lived billions of years ago, we can reason in an analogical way that modern slime molds are a living example of the early steps in biological organization, perhaps an example of the continuous chain of evolution toward the human mind, a "pre-enactment" as Peter Dawkins puts it, of our present metazoan multicellularity, complexity, and behavior.

These Myxomycetes demonstrate a remarkable degree of organization that works for their survival and propagation. They may have evolved—somewhere between one and two bya—from ancient protobacteria. The amoeboid slime mold cells grow and divide as individuals, close to but independent of each other, devouring rotting vegetation and animal feces. When the food supply diminishes, the cells transmit chemical signals to each other, the wave of communication flowing like a ripple through the water, triggering the cells to transform themselves into a colony, a "single, multicellular organism." This slug-like organism moves until it finds a more favorable location for survival and nourishment. It then develops stalks, sporangia, containing clusters of spores, that are released, spread, and germinate into individual slime mold cells that begin this process over again.[68]

The ability of these amoeboid cells to organize into a single motile organism suggests an inherent high level of awareness and intention, and represents a sort of thinking through a primordial communicating system of the simplest of eukaryotes.

The behavior of other simple organisms in our living universe also helps to illuminate our understanding of this evolutionary process. The paramecium, in contrast with the ameba, can be observed over reasonably short time-spans because of the rapid movements produced from its ciliated surface. Its motion may appear erratic but, as one of our greatest theoretical physicists, Nobel laureate Richard Feynman, pointed out, the behavior may not be random but purposeful. The conjugation of two paramecia to exchange nuclei, and their behavior when dehydrating, due to environmental changes, into a "seed," seem indeed to represent complex processes. Feynman said, "Until we see how many dimensions of behavior even a one-celled animal has, we won't be able to fully understand the behavior of more complicated animals."[69] Perhaps recent studies showing the remarkable learning capacities of single specialized cells, such as mammalian neurons, will help put us on the track to answering Feynman's challenge of nearly twenty years ago.

The process of evolution that shaped the "complex interrelationship of all living and non-living things," according to former U.S. Vice President Al Gore, may be understandable scientifically, "But the simple fact of the living world and our place on it awakes awe, wonder, a sense of mystery—a spiritual response—when one reflects on its inner meaning."[70] And it is that spiritual connection that is in danger of withering as we turn our backs on our only friend, the biosphere.

GAIA

WINTER REVERIE ABOUT A LIVING EARTH

L OW BANKS OF madder, purple, and orange along the horizon festoon the white-gray edges of the snow-clad city. There is a slow and majestic change of color. The oranges darken, the purples become blues, and the spectrum shifts as the yellowing solar orb sinks to the other side of the world. My imagination shifts its orientation. The sun does not sink; I am standing on a spinning sphere, rotating away from our begetter, the energy source of life, and I hope it will spin long enough to return to that nourishing, enlightening benevolence by morning.

The long line of clouds darkens. I must have seen nearly every color there is to see in the past half-hour. The looming shadows are outlined by fiery crimson haloes, glowing with hues of magenta and lilac. Behind them float iridescent streaks blushing with ochre and saffron. The backdrop to all is infinite space tinted with azure merging through turquoise and amber to the rubiginous strand where the atmosphere curves down to coat the global surface.

How many such scenes have happened since our beginnings in the primordial sea? They were often surely beyond imagination—cataclysmic eruptions, violent storms of hot gases and steam, showers of pumice and rain, all faithfully recorded by the eternal laws of prismatic optics; each speck and droplet in the atmosphere providing the necessary light-bending surface to evoke every hue of every color that our retina perceives. Every evening in every part of our mother planet when the sun was visible, that scene was repeated for billions of years in every conceivable variety of chromatic glory. The earliest life sensed it. Did ancestral organisms adopt part of the brilliance of these ancient meteorological displays? I look at flowers and birds, gaze over a verdant valley in springtime and see that the spectrum of color that living things have appropriated is like the changing sunset. In the fading glory of this winter gloaming I see a part of me that bathed in the same radiance billions of years ago.

🐟

One astronaut, viewing Earth's atmosphere from space, was "terrified by its fragile appearance."[71] "We all live in a subjective and fragile soap bubble," according to the pioneering German ecologist Jacob von Uexkuell.[72] This is not just a poetic impression. Underneath us is the cooled and hardened shell of our Earth, just about 48 miles thick at the most, and only about 4 miles thick in places below the ocean floors. We float on that thin shell over a gigantic core of increasingly molten magma, 4,000 degrees Centigrade in its center, on a veritable crust that shields us from extinction. Around us is the biosphere, a relatively thin sheet of water, land, and air that supports life. From the deepest parts of our oceans to the limits of sustainable life in the high atmosphere, the biosphere is no thicker than perhaps 11 miles, the distance that an automobile can travel in a few minutes or a champion runner can achieve in less than an hour.[73] Yet well over ninety percent of all life dwells in an even thinner layer, only about 4 miles thick when bisected by the ocean level. That is just the distance of a brisk morning walk!

If we imagine that Earth is reduced to the size of a large orange, then the equivalent thickness of the biosphere becomes approximately that of a sheet of thick writing paper.[74] The volume of the biosphere relative to that of Earth is less than one-tenth of one percent. The tenuous state of this thin sheet of our biosphere is experienced, for example, when seismic events occur. These can be relatively small shifts in the Earth's cooling crust, yet, as was seen in the Indian Ocean tsunami of 2004, can lead to forces that swept away tens of thousands of human and other lives in a matter of minutes. Within this biosphere, however, are incredible forces of life that have created millions of species and incalculable numbers of living organisms.

The concept that our Earth is a living, homeostatic organism led the English biologist James Lovelock to give our planet the name *Gaia,* after the Greek name for the Earth and its goddess.[75] Earlier, however, the priest and philosopher Pierre Teilhard de Chardin postulated that intelligence pervading the cosmos had led to the evolution of life on Earth into a "single, giant organism" that he called Demeter.[76] Even before these visionaries, great minds such as Aristotle and Gustav Fechner conceived the very same thing. Vast dynamic forces have often prevailed to counter the natural destructive activities that this planet has experienced over billions of years. For example, biospheric homeostasis, what today we call the "Gaia effect," appears to have adjusted carbon dioxide levels to less than half of that predicted several decades ago for the present time. This is probably due to its increased utilization by plants as its availability increases with global warming. Plants will grow and proliferate more under those conditions. Furthermore, temperate forests are regrowing. In New Hampshire, where ninety-five percent of the land was covered by forest in 1680, only fifteen percent remained forested in 1880, yet now the forest has returned to cover eighty-five percent.

Yet still the urbanization of the world is leading populations away from the sacredness of Nature—or even awareness of it. That source of mystical inspiration is increasingly denied to vast numbers. What is left in its place? The ecologist Roger Gottlieb urges that this spiritual connection should not just affect us, but should "inhabit and shape us." An "enzyme of consciousness" could expand environmental awareness in many ways: translating theory to strategy, shifting the focus from physical to biological priorities, and exploring the meaning of nature's divinity as a forum of "eco-theology," which could expand the boundaries of what modern humanity has considered as sacred.

BIOPHILIA

Around me, in a forest, in a handful of soil, in the rivers and ponds, are living cells, alone or joined as individuals of various sizes and complexities—a throbbing pulse of life, all related to me through that common ancestor, the veritable Adam of Creation, a speck of protoplasm. I feel at home and in tune. Ralph Waldo Emerson in his first book, *Nature,* wrote, "The greatest delight which the fields and woods minister is the suggestion of an occult relation between man and vegetable. I am not alone and unacknowledged. They nod to me, and I to them."[77] In Wordsworth's *Tintern Abbey,* the poet speaks of the mystical kinship between nature and the human spirit and of the "power of harmony...as we see into the life of things." That harmony relates to "the innate tendency to focus on life and lifelike processes" that the Harvard entomologist Edward O. Wilson defines as biophilia.

Since our evolution parallels that of all other present life, then our whole being, physical and psychic, has developed over eons of close proximity to other life, and even to its incorporation into our very cells. This association, Wilson asserts, results in an inherited attraction to nature and fellow life. In our psyche we contain engrams (neural connections) for coexistence, but also for competition and exploitation. All our concepts of beauty, pleasure, fear, distaste, and attraction are based upon the inheritance of these engrams. In an example, the passionate feelings for life and nature of Richard Jeffries, the nineteenth-century English mystic, vividly express the deep roots of biophilia and its mystical connection:

> Touching the crumble of earth, and blade of grass, the thyme flower, breathing the earth-encircling air, thinking of the sea and sky, holding out my hand for the sunbeams to touch it, prone on the sward in token of deep reverence, thus I prayed that I might touch to the unutterable existence infinitely higher than deity.[78]

What would any human being be without life around us, if only crows in a congested city or companionable dogs or sparse strips of vegetation, not only for physical survival but for spiritual nourishment? We form ties of affection spontaneously with both plants and animals, and these feelings can profoundly affect us. The poet Rilke wrote of flowers "faithful to earthliness" while mankind, weighty and pleased by his gravitas, presumes to instruct them, yet,

> O how lightly he'd emerge
> From the depth they had shared, different into a different day,
> Or maybe he'd stay; and they'd blossom and extol
> Him as someone converted, resembling now one of their own,
> All the silent siblings in the breeze of the meadow.[79]

I watch homeless men and women sitting in a square, feeding pigeons. I feel their pleasure of contact with other living creatures. Look at the aquariums in doctors' waiting rooms, containing graceful, colorful fish that solace anxious patients. There are now even "healing gardens," like the Howard Ulfelder Healing Garden atop the massive, impersonal structures of the Massachusetts General Hospital in Boston, designed to comfort and support the sick. Contact with living beings is an obvious human need. A quarter of a million Americans are said to be devoted birdwatchers, and millions watch whales each year.[80]

There is no reason to believe that these engrams have been lost over the brief evolutionary history of modern Homo. But, as the ecologist and philosopher David Abram points out, inherited patterns must be adapted to the immediate situation of our orientation in the present world. Our ability to process sensory stimuli may atrophy from disuse; though we see and hear with beautifully evolved sets of eyes and ears, the messages to the brain may be blurred or simply lost.

Most of us are oblivious to much of Nature's language. If, as Abram says, "we no longer experience the enveloping Earth as expressive and alive," then our senses have gone somewhere else. It is "the written text" that now speaks to us instead. "The stones fall silent, the trees become mute, the animals dumb."[81]

With the specter of global urbanization threatening to deny whole generations of populations any animal contact save pigeons and pets, I have a foreboding feeling of fragmentation of the collective psyche. With each succeeding generation cut off from nature, there is, inevitably, a process that the psychologist Peter Kahn calls "environmental degradation": a loss of experience, and thus a progressive depletion of the memory of our connection with nature.[82] The disappearance of the "wild others," as Paul Shepard sees it, leaves nothing but our own image to explain ourselves, leaving an empty psychic space.[83]

True, millions of species have come and gone on this planet. What, really, is the difference if this or that animal or plant disappears forever. Will it be our turn soon?

There is an ongoing debate about what biophilia means and if it exists. Is it inherited or acquired? Edward Wilson believes that it is a fundamental, inherited need to affiliate with nature, a magnetic polarization drawing us back to our roots. I suggest that it can be a limitless, seamless sense of attachment to all creation, an innate spiritual feeling for all being, call it nature or call it God.

Is urbanization crushing out the last vestiges of topophilia and biophilia? I sometimes think so when talking to city dwellers that are either totally enchanted with their concrete environment or beset by crowding, poverty, and strife.

One tiny example of how humanity can nurture its tenuous connection with nature from its concrete warrens of urban life is the zoological park. People need to see, smell, and possibly touch their fellow animal beings, for example in children's "petting" zoos. There are even "therapy" animals, meant to be held, petted, and loved by disturbed and disadvantaged individuals.

It is remarkable where one finds zoos. There are flea-infested, decrepit zoos in remote cities of developing countries where urban sprawl, poverty and overcrowding have blocked out all contact with nature. At the ethical cost of removing wildlife from its natural habitat, these dusty places, often poorly run with dismayingly inhumane conditions for the animals, still may provide some experience of the innate love we have for fellow life.

It is sad, indeed, to capture and imprison wildlife for the sake of human pleasure. Sadder is the fact that we often capture them in order to preserve species endangered by our subconscious yet relentless elbowing aside of fellow inhabitants of this Earth.

The loss of wildlife, not just the "charismatic" big mammals, but "all creatures great and small," plants and trees as well, leads to a spiritually sterile world. Our love of plants, stemming from what the American naturalist and ecologist Paul Shepard calls *phytoresonance* "a resonance to which we are intrinsically predisposed and psychologically committed by our ontogeny,"[84] moves us to try in gardens as well as zoos to capture a bit of the primeval forest and evoke our ancient roots. The Oriental garden, for example, is a contemplative garden, a place of healing, refuge, and homage to this Earth. The Zen garden particularly brings out mystical feelings that can lead to the sense of unity with nature. This formal creation presents an opportunity for unhindered meditation.

From a different perspective, however, the Oriental garden is a stunted and artificial substitute for nature. When viewed within the framework of certain traditions and cultures it is beautiful and enriching to the spirit. When seen by a native of the Amazon forest, it may seem to be a view of nature in prison.

Nature means space. As the English psychiatrist Anthony Stevens has reported, restriction of that space can play murderous havoc within a baboon population, and other data support this behavior in other species such as rodents crowded in cages. The philosopher and ethologist Desmond Morris has "compared our (the human) lot to that of animals condemned to languish in a zoo of their own making."[85]

A notorious example of cultural breakdown and degeneration among human beings was reported by the anthropologist C. M. Turnbull. After being forced off their hunting territory and into farming, the Ik tribe of Uganda transformed into an "irrevocably disagreeable collection of unattached, brutish creatures."[86] Among other Swiftian perversions, they defecated on their neighbors' doorsteps. Cities and nations have adopted some Ik-like characteristics. It is perhaps a form of spiritual decompensation demonstrated by a loss of natural habitat and the pollution of streets, water, and atmosphere.

The movement of humanity into urban settings, which furthers the alienation from nature, may lead to other disturbing consequences. Life in nature had dangers and unexpected changes that kept our forebears watchful and humble. The Swiss psychiatrist C. A. Meier views this transition to a more "civilized" society from a Jungian perspective. He believes that as the fears of outer natural dangers turn inward, Western society will approach a crisis from the fears of the inner dangers in the psyche, "for should the outer wilderness disappear altogether, it would inevitably resurrect powerfully from within, whereupon it would immediately be projected."[87] We are seeing a resurgence of those inward projections as humanity festers in a global psychosis of internecine crises—as seen in the increasing worldwide incidence of mental illness reported by the World Health Organization.

We can work for sanity by recognizing that humanity is not a unique example of life on this planet. Rather, we are all part of an evolving genetic and psychic continuum reaching back to the primeval sources of our ancestry. In our communion with the natural world through mystic experience, we may also be connecting with ancient sources that link us with all life on Earth. One such connection that is discussed in the next chapter is our heritage as a hunting society.

3. The Hunter

"Hunting is the master behavior pattern of the human species."
WILLIAM LAUGHLIN, *Culture: Man's Adaptive Dimension*

"For perhaps ninety-five percent of our history we have been primarily hunters."
PAUL SHEPARD, *Encounters with Nature*

AN ANGLER'S TRANCE

I STOOD ALONE IN the water near the bank from where I had emerged. All was still. The ripples from the disturbance of my boots smoothed into the blank mirror of water. A bird called in the distance. Murmurs of distant rapids sounded. Creaks and crackles came from the growth along the riverbank. A bubbling of life seemed to emerge from every speck of earth, every drop of water, every breath of air. Roiling thoughts of problems lingering from where I had come quickly faded. My attention turned to that moment of dawn upon a river tracking a quarry. The surrounding sky, hills, trees, and water merged in my inner vision to a brilliant panorama. In a moment the whole world entered my spirit together with the stars and galaxies still glimmering in the light of dawn and all the limitless space beyond.

My mind was now blank, yet each sense was sharply aware of all about me—every sound, every movement, and every smell. The Earth slowly awakened—more scraping in the bush, birdcalls, the hum of insects, and the faint rattle of leaves from a gentle movement of air. Smells of rotting vegetation and wild roses drifted by in the slow breeze. Time was forgotten. The sky lightened and the stars and galaxies faded from sight. There was a splash from the distant bank, and a muskrat with its whiskered seal head erect swam by without the slightest notice of my still solitary figure. A dimple appeared ahead on the placid water.

I was aware of all, yet my eyes rested on that one spot. The dimple reappeared. After long experience, I knew not to think. I slowly raised the rod, ran out line, and cast the curling line with its passenger, the feathered hook. I carried out the movement on command from an inner source that was always and solely the source of certainty. The fly gently landed one foot to the right and one foot upstream of the dimple pattern. There was a sudden swirl of water, the tranquility of that pastoral picture disappeared, and the spell was gone.

The Alert Human

Until about ten thousand years ago (an iota of evolution) we were all hunters and foragers, living in daily intimacy with all surrounding life.[88] It is small wonder then that hunting stirs deep recesses in our consciousness and brings up a sharp awareness of this connection. Over the thousands of centuries of modern Homo's development, alertness was a prime necessity, for both attack and defense. That awareness can still result in a vibrant state in which all senses become more acute, and time and space merge into a feeling of unity.

The Spanish philosopher José Ortega y Gasset, in *Meditations on Hunting,* describes the state of awareness in what we know as the "hunter's trance":

> He [the hunter] does not look tranquilly in one determined direction, sure beforehand that the game will pass in front of him. The hunter knows that he does not know what is going to happen, and that is one of the greatest attractions of his

occupation. Thus he needs to prepare an attention of a different and superior style—an attention that does not consist in riveting itself in the presumed but consists precisely in not presuming anything and avoiding inattentiveness. It is a "universal" attention, which does not inscribe itself in any point and tries to be on all points. There is a magnificent term for this, one that still conserves all the zest of vivacity and imminence: alertness. The hunter is the alert man.[89]

Ortega y Gasset associated the development of the capacities of observation and alertness in the ancient hunter to the evolution of the intellect.[90] Today, the sensory processes many traditional hunters still possess are, to us, extraordinary—yet we must once have possessed them, too. Every aspect of life and environment (weather, geology, and geography) has been part of the lives of these peoples for tens of thousands of years, and the traditional hunter has a mystical connection not only with the quarry, but also with his environment. Henry David Thoreau observed fellow fishermen on Walden Pond, "as wise in natural lore as the citizen is in artificial. They never consulted with books, and know and tell much less then they have done. The things which they practice are said not yet to be known."[91]

A Hunter's Trance

A hunting friend described his experience of stalking Wapiti elk in Colorado:

> One day in May I set out at dawn, alone, to track elk. There was still plenty of snow and muddy terrain to follow the herds migrating to upland pasture. I came across fresh tracks of several elk, including one bull. The morning was bright and sunny with a slight wind in my face, assuring me of getting a reasonably close approach to my quarry. After perhaps an hour of slow and careful tracking, I came out on a long glade, fifty yards wide. If the elk were nearby they would detect my

crossing the snowy and slushy meadow. It remained for me to be completely still and pay complete attention to the opposite hillside. I felt now their presence and somehow knew that they felt mine. As I stood there, the sense of time remarkably changed. What seemed like minutes I found later to have been over an hour. An intense feeling of the clarity of the scene swept over me. All my senses seemed to sharpen to an exquisite razor's edge. I heard the tiniest sounds of distant streams and rustling leaves as if magnified in a celestial amplifier. Everything seemed closer to me and I felt, amazingly, a sort of merger of myself with everything, a sense of belongingness. I was connected with everything in that panorama, the grass, trees, rocks, insects, birds, the elk that I knew were quietly moving uphill, out of my sights. I felt a great rush of emotion, a joy at being alive, the chance to exist along with everything else. I will never forget that day. What happened to the elk? I never saw them.

The hunter's unfocused alertness, his trance, is similar to the attentive form of meditation practiced in Zen Buddhism.[92] The word *trance* means precisely what the Latin roots say: *trans* (across) *ire* (go)—to move across, to pass over to the object. One's whole being is directed toward a quarry; one is alert with "universal attention," unfocused, aware of all yet somehow filtering out what is extraneous or irrelevant. The blocking or diversion of those external and internal signals sharpens his senses.

This state of mind, then, is not unique to the hunter; E. O. Wilson, searching the jungle floor for his entomologist's quarry in the first pages of this book, experienced an intensification of his concentration, and the physiological changes of respiration and heartbeat, as the transcendent trance swept across his senses. It is a phenomenon common to many who search and is, as Ortega y Gasset maintains, the ground for the creative process. The external world as perceived by the hunter is drawn into his inner vision, which leads to a feeling of union with all that is outside, in fact, the cosmos.

In my outwardly casual interviews with fellow hunters and anglers I find a spectrum of comments on what constitutes the hunter's trance. Some describe a simple focus upon tracking the quarry, akin perhaps to the tiger stalking and preparing to dispatch his prey. From others, I hear of feelings of unity with nature or the cosmos, of alterations in the sense of time and light, of unforgettable moments.

The Zen practice of *shikan-taza* resembles the hunter's trance in that the mind is brought to a heightened state of awareness, intensely involved in the object of its attention. *Shikan-taza* is a ritual of mental preparation for *bushido,* or actual battle, but could as well be part of the stalking hunt. Yet, simultaneously, participants can be peculiarly relaxed and detached, centered into the ground of their own being. This acute sensitivity of awareness lies at the heart of a mystical state from which energy can flow into extraordinary physical and mental achievement. But Zen practitioners and the stalking hunter know that such concentration is only possible over short periods of time, perhaps half an hour or so.

This inner preparation for the hunt, tied through evolution to the drive to find, to discover, and ultimately to create, is a meditative state preparing an individual for "the path found when one falls into the 'Naturalist's trance,' the hunter's pursuit of wild game, the curandera's search for hidden roots, the fisherman's casting of the net into the current, the water witcher's trust of the forked willow branch, the rock climber's fixation on the slightest details of a cliff face." Naturalist Gary Paul Nabhan asks, "Why is it that when we are hanging from the cliff—beyond the reach of civilization's safety net...we are most likely to gain the deepest sense of what it is to be alive?"[93]

Alertness and awareness hone the consciousness. And, where it is a matter of life or death, they are factors of evolutionary selection. Hunting, including foraging and exploration for new territory, has been perhaps a vital factor in the development of humankind's mind, speech, and much of early human culture.[94]

Stalking a quarry evokes those qualities of alertness and connectiveness that tune the brain to a high pitch, a pure vibration of total

awareness. Watch a cat on the stalk in the garden, or, if you are fortu-
nate enough to be Jim Corbett, a tiger in its forest. The perfect concentration of that feline belies its total awareness of everything around it.
See the ears quiver and turn with each sound. The quarry, if aware of its
predator, may be equally alert in playing its role in the deadly game.

The stalking tiger, David Peat observes, is a pure example of
perception and awareness.[95] Contrast this with the way most people
live, their senses numbed and alienated from their environment. The
quality of primal alertness can, however, be recaptured.

I know a master hunter, a hunter of fish, whom I described in
Revenge of the Fishgod:

> His slow and stealthy approach was that of a stalking Indian
> hunter.... The stalking approach...came from very primitive
> instincts. The concentration focused upon the quarry was
> absolute—the Hunter's Trance. A half-hour could elapse with-
> out movement or any thought, only total absorption upon the
> slightest activity from underwater. The mind was remarkably
> cleared of extraneous cerebral noise.[96]

Christopher Camuto in his evocative book on nature and hunting
writes of "dreamlike moments" occurring during the "transcendental
concentration of the hunt."[97] The hunter's trance is thus a form of
meditation, but in a dynamic and primal mode that evolved from
evolutionary forces that existed millions years ago.

Many professional hunters support the theory that there is an
inborn instinct for hunting.[98] In *Woman the Hunter,* Mary Stange
observes that men, women, and children, when newly introduced to
the stalking of game, become "visibly changed, their pace becoming
more stealthy and deliberate, their breathing and facial expressions
altered." The hunting guide sees that those "who had never hunted
before had all the instinctive movements that many people think they
learn only through years of experience."[99]

The animal tracker Paul Rezendes regards stalking as a form
of walking meditation, yet "all the while being incredibly attentive

and aware of everything around you."[100] The hunter's pursuit of his prey may involve every resource: physical, mental, and spiritual. Jim Corbett's accounts of tracking and killing the man-eaters of the Himalayan Terrai convey the total involvement necessary when nearly equal adversaries contend. Corbett was raised in the landscape of northern India and absorbed the rhythms and sensations of forest and stream, the lore and myth of animals.[101] His solitary quests are prime examples of "stalking meditation," an acute state of concentration in which the stalker moves from "the tiny perspective of self" to an "awareness with the eyes of the whole universe."[102] It is as if one's perceptiveness were honed, like a razor, to an unimaginable acuity.

What primitive instincts do we retain to help us cope with utter wilderness or with circumstances that detract us from orientation even in the midst of civilization? Erik Jonsson, a Swedish engineer and outdoorsman, believes that people do retain an inner compass but that the confusion of being hemmed in by artificial distractions throws off the natural sense of orientation. Since several primitive species, such as mollusks, crustaceans, insects, frogs, newts, and fishes, have a magnetic sense, then it is likely, Jonsson reasons, that a primitive ancestor of ours also had a magnetic sense. This ability would not have disappeared as we evolved, unless there was a long period when we did not use it. He believes that it is highly probable that we still have a magnetic sense to fall back on when there are no outer cues for direction.[103]

I can argue, however, that there are always clues for direction in nature. The senses, if they are acute enough, will detect the very slightest cue: a breeze, a change of temperature, of light, of terrain, sky, or stars.

When all conditions in our inner and outer selves are in harmony, the senses that connect us to the outside may lead, through neural pathways, straight into an inner realm of our consciousness of which, as William James implied, we are normally scarcely aware. Seeing with that inner eye and with every sense of our nervous system allows us to perceive, equally for the thinker, hunter, poet and artist, a grand and sweeping landscape that transcends our usual waking consciousness.

This happened one spring evening when the New England nature writer John Hay watched for hours a poppy closing its petals. That long and focused mental devolution, a naturalist's trance, led Hay to a heavenly unity: "By then I had become part of a whole new cosmos, barely glimpsed, a new opening into space and time and into feeling. I had never thought of sense perception in a flower."[104] Hay had surely formed a spiritual bond with that solitary plant. The outer eye becomes the inner eye; awareness expands into a vast dimension, encompassing one's total being and all one's surroundings.

Annie Dillard in her classic *Pilgrim at Tinker Creek* stalks to observe, not to kill; yet she hunts with the same mind as our ancestral alert man.

> In summer, I stalk. Summer leaves obscure, heat dazzles, and creatures hide from the red-eyed sun, and me. I have to seek things out. The creatures I seek have several senses and free will; it becomes apparent that they do not wish to be seen. I can stalk them in either of two ways. The first is not what you think of as true stalking, but it is the *via negativa,* and as fruitful as actual pursuit. When I stalk this way I take my stand on a bridge and wait, emptied. I put myself in the way of the creature's passage, like spring Eskimos at a seal's breathing hole. Something might come, something might go. I am Newton under the apple tree, Buddha under the Bo.[105]

When Dillard stands on the bridge, "emptied," it is the same as preparing for meditation. The mind is made receptive. Either deliberately or subconsciously, thoughts are quenched, and sensory input is enhanced through this clearing of neural pathways, Zen meditation and other "altered states of consciousness" that I have presented all lead to an "emptying," or *via negativa,* that opens the mind to enhanced perception, be it of a quarry, a unity with the universe, or God.

Another hunter was Vladimir Nabokov, an avid lepidopterist. He vividly records his lifelong passion of capturing, killing, mounting, and classifying moths and butterflies in page after page of his autobiography. Perhaps as with other hunters and anglers, this hobby was in part driven by the primitive undercurrent of the hunt, to embrace the mystical comfort of nature. Other great writers of that land have also lovingly described the Russian landscape, particularly before the Revolution. Nabokov returns again and again to his childhood memories of Russia's forests, fields, and streams. As with others, his mystical experience included a sense of timelessness. As he wanders across the fields, stalking his winged prey, this feeling appears, and he exclaims, "This is ecstasy, and behind ecstasy is something else, which is hard to explain. It is like a momentary vacuum into which rushes all that I love. A sense of oneness with sun and stone."[106] He captures the feeling of apophasis, of an emptiness that is a boundless receptacle for creative energy, and the cosmic unity that is represented by love, the ground of being.

We need not, of course, stalk an animal quarry. Mushroom hunting may serve the purpose. Ultimately a solitary walk in the woods with no purpose in mind yet with primal alertness can lead to the same union with our Mother Nature that has been so often described by writers and poets. It is likely, however, that evolutionary changes have inserted the hunting instinct into our genome. That instinct can serve to discover a new species, a new mineral, and a new part of this Earth or beyond. In the film *A River Runs Through It,* the protagonist's father reminds him, "All there is to thinking—is seeing something you weren't noticing which makes you see something that isn't even visible."[107] Thus Newton and the apple, Buddha under the Bo.

THE ARCHER AND THE INNER GAME

It is not coincidental that archery, and other martial arts such as *bushido,* have been adopted in Zen and other Eastern philosophies as exercises of the mind and body to approach the mystical state of *satori,* a state of enlightenment. It can be imagined that the formalization of these hunting and martial arts into disciplines of meditation and perfection of living began with rituals early in our evolution. Paleolithic cave art suggests that these states of union with the quarry extended beyond our historical reach.

The German philosophy professor Eugen Herrigel spent years in Japan learning the art of archery from Zen teachers. At the point of achieving mastery of the bow, Herrigel felt a sudden jolt of concentration that seemed to remove the block, or inhibition, that had long beset him. It occurred spontaneously, and once that barrier was surmounted, Herrigel knew that the flight of the arrow to the true mark could be repeated with certainty.

Indeed, the condition of alertness is key to Zen philosophy and to its forms of discipline and exercise. The fine line where a transcendental experience appears is beautifully expressed when Herrigel makes that leap through the invisible wall as he continues:

> With its help the soul is brought to the point where it vibrates
> of itself in itself—a serene pulsation, which can be heightened
> into the feeling, otherwise experienced only in rare dreams, of
> extraordinary lightness, and the rapturous certainty of being
> able to summon up energies in any direction, to intensify or to
> release tensions graded to nicety.[108]

Christopher Camuto, preparing for the hunt, experienced this leap of concentration. The critical point in his training in marksmanship was when "every muscle in your body shifts to serve that aim." His experience is like Herrigel's: "You can feel the body and mind come together, and the arrow flies straight to the spot without your having a conscious memory of releasing it." Ultimately he realizes that the bowman is a passive onlooker, "egoless," releasing the arrow, not shooting it, and when mind and body are perfectly coordinated the arrow will go exactly to its goal.[109]

This essence of Zen is illustrated in what we might call the "angler's trance," by the perfect cast to the hidden quarry, a mindless yet intricately coordinated motion that is beyond instinct and beyond conscious purposeful action.

There is an "inner" game throughout the spectrum of arts and sports. Take for instance a highly technical form of mountaineering called bouldering. Here John Gill describes the mystical dimensions of "inner" climbing where the boulderer finds self-realization through kinesthetic awareness. Beyond the barriers of demanding technical moves, the pain and uncertainty, there remains the exhilarating and fundamental quality called inner climbing. "If one never proceeds beyond these barriers, no matter what the limits of one's technical competence, the ecstasy of artistic fulfillment is never captured."

Just as Herrigel repetitively practiced archery until an invisible wall was suddenly transcended, so can this magic occur to the boulderer, as Gill writes: "To saturate the mind with kinaesthetic awareness is to enter a state of reality in which grace and precision define the world."[110] The boulderer, too, sees the rock as his prey, to which he is physically and spiritually bound.

The hunter's trance is thus a total mental and physical concentration whereby extraneous signals, internal or external, are quenched or diverted, enabling the psyche of the hunter to perceive his quarry and its world with a supernormal alertness. The merging of that world into the mind allows the subject to experience a comprehension that extends beyond the everyday dimensions of perception. It is, in fact, a form of meditation that probes the subconscious. The subject thus feels a harmony, a unity, a merging of Self with object, the quarry, and its surroundings. As we will see, the neural pathways of the limbic system may play a major role in this and other mystical experiences. What remains beyond reductive analysis is the particular affinity of the hunter with the inanimate and inorganic world from which we have evolved. This is the true mystical connection with Gaia.

4. The Warrior and Athlete

"Strife is the source and master of all things."

HERACLITUS

"You will recall, if you saw the film *Patton,* the scene in which the American general, who commanded the Third Army in the 1944–45 drive across France into Germany, walks across the field after a battle: churned earth, burnt tanks, dead men. The general takes up a dying officer, kisses him, surveys the havoc, and says: 'I love it. God help me, I do so love it. I love it more than my life.'"

JAMES HILLMAN, *A Blue Fire*[111]

WAR AS A MYSTICAL EXPERIENCE

MAN'S HERITAGE AS a hunter is closely connected to his role as warrior, defending or seeking his own family and territory. Human nature is competitive, and our genes have not changed significantly in the past fifty thousand years; our history and mythology are full of war. The Jungian psychologist James Hillman wrote: "The monumental epics that lie in the roots of our Western languages are to a large proportion 'war books': the Mahabharata and its Bhagavad Gita, the Iliad, the Aenead, the Celtic Lebor Gabala, and the Norse Edda. Our Bible is a long account of battles, of wars and captains of wars."[112]

In the midst of war there can come mystical experiences that hark back to our primeval past—where nothing veiled the stark realities of strife and the visions of imminent death. Similarly to the cinematic and the real-life Patton, Pierre Teilhard de Chardin, who served as a medical orderly in World War I, described his "nostalgia for the front," in which "for a moment they [his comrades] knew real emotions, they were united, they were raised above themselves." He recalls moments at time of war that gave a sense of "rising to a higher level of human existence."[113]

The duty to do battle lies near the deep heart of our origins; the struggle to survive is inescapable. In the Bhagavad Gita, Lord Krishna speaks of a perpetual and eternal energy that demands action, the compelling call to duty that summons the warrior prince Arjuna to gird himself in battle against a foe that includes family and friends. Krishna tells Arjuna, "Perform every action with your heart fixed on the Supreme Lord.... Renounce attachment to the fruits," and "Look to your own duty; do not tremble before it; nothing is better for a warrior than a battle of sacred duty."[114] The Gita remains a profound statement of the universality of strife and of the call for transcendental resolutions of human fears and conflicts.

Joan of Arc and Florence Nightingale, T. E. Lawrence, and Generals Orde Wingate, "Chinese" Gordon, and Patton were among many mystics of war and suffering, battle and death. Evelyn Underhill writes of a "true and virile" mysticism that emerges in time of war:

> We, horrified by the external circumstances, the devastation, the misery and evil, know little of the spiritual drama which is brought so far into being by the present war [1914–1918]. But in so far as we accept the mystic belief, and where there is suffering, difficulty and effort, and this is met by loyalty and courage, there is always hope. This war, thus regarded, is a crucible for souls.[115]

Lamentable though the circumstances may be, in deadly conflict primitive neurophysiological mechanisms mobilize the individual for "fight or flight." The surge of enkephalins such as endorphins and other neurotransmitters in the limbic system undoubtedly induces a tranquility and hyperawareness that are also important evolutionary coping mechanisms for survival.

The memories of such encounters, as reported by those surviving close battle, match the feelings of explorers, mountaineers, and others facing the looming tensions of danger, or of athletes in the stresses of competition. These feelings are frequently colloquially labeled "highs" and often include all the criteria that William James listed for mystical experience.

TRANSCENDENTAL ATHLETICS

From the practices of war and hunting there developed competitive sports exercises and ultimately athletics (from the Greek *athlein*, to contend for a prize). It is logical to suppose that our competitive traits stem from the genes associated with hunting instincts that evolved with increasing brain size. Our psychic connection with the quarry, developed through extreme concentration and effort, applies as well to the opponent, the target, the goal.

"I was playing out of my mind!" One hears this often from athletes. It indicates awareness that the thinking mind is not the controlling force in the intricate coordination of muscular power and neurological signals needed in an athletic achievement.

The terms "flow," "groove," "zone," and "high" are associated with athletics. They denote ecstatic experiences, characterized, no matter what the sport, by feelings of effortlessness, acute intuition, and strange calmness,[116] with a sense of altered time (namely slow motion) and frequently enhanced luminosity, including auras and haloes.[117] Many of these experiences relate to extreme physical stress, a known factor in the increased activity of enkephalins in the brain, but other mechanisms, some still not understood, are significant. For example, as with Herrigel's study of archery (chapter 3), extreme repetitious practice in order to hone muscular strength and coordination,

coupled with the seemingly paradoxical combination of concentration and detachment of the mind, can enable the athlete, just like the
hunter, to experience an expansion of his awareness that permits him
to perform extraordinary feats.

One of my own experiences strikingly supports the existence of
those magical moments. I participated once in a sailing race near
San Diego. The day was windy with a driving fog. We dodged in
and out of several banks of opaque mist and emerged suddenly into
bright sunlight. There, a few boat lengths ahead we were startled to
see several competitors charging on a collision course with us. The
situation demanded lightning decisions. Throughout the race I had
been anxious about skippering my friend's thirty-five-foot sloop. At
that moment of crisis, suddenly and miraculously, I experienced
a unique calmness and clarity of vision. The entire scene took on
an enhanced brightness, time seemed to slow down, and the noise
of the commotion of shouting sailors, surging waves, and slatting
sails faded. A rush of confidence replaced anxiety. The crew looked
back anxiously, awaiting orders. I gave them; we maneuvered with
a few feet of safety to spare. We finished the race and the sensation
was forgotten until much later when I began to ponder this strange
experience.

I am not usually a person who copes well in crisis. I seem to require
precious time to think out the best course of action. In this incident it
seemed as if some greater power inside me had suddenly appeared to
cope with the crisis and then, just as suddenly, had disappeared.

Andrew Cooper, writing on sports, emphasizes that this "self-
transcendence" (the most profound characteristic of playing "in
the zone") cannot be produced by force of will. "If the Self tries to
go beyond itself it just creates more Self."[118] In fact a self-conscious
attempt to go beyond these limits may result in the paralytic disaster
of "choking," a condition well known to most athletes and also public speakers.

Perceptive observers often appreciate these transcendent moments
in athletes. In the Wimbledon tennis matches on July 4, 2001, the

sports commentator described the player Roger Federer as being "in the zone.... His appearance is calm, remote, untouched by the crowd's or opponent's emotions, and he is creating amazing shots." This remarkable player continues to display an inner calm and strength of demeanor in his matches.

Herbert Benson reports a quotation by a tennis player who once described "the zone" as "so complete and intense that it evoked a state of almost semiconscious euphoria—one that many believe bears a resemblance to hypnosis, and enables a top player to achieve his or her peak performance."[119]

The first person to run a four-minute mile, Roger Bannister, wrote, "The earth seemed almost to move with me. I was running— and a fresh rhythm entered my body. No longer conscious of my movement, I discovered a new unity of nature. I had found a new source of power and beauty, a source I never dreamt existed—."[120]

The Russian weight lifter Yuri Vlasov noted:

> While the blood is pounding in your head, all suddenly becomes quiet within you. At that moment you have the conviction that you contain all the power in the world, that you are capable of everything, that you have wings. There is no more precious moment in life than this...and you will work very hard for years just to taste it again.[121]

Long-distance running, whether alone or in competition, is associated with many accounts of ecstatic experience. "Runner's high" is now a well-known term, connoting a euphoric feeling that occurs well into a run. After thirty minutes of running, says long-distance runner Valerie Andrews, there comes a renewed energy and relaxing of the brain's censoring device. "Thoughts and feelings pour out uninhibited by the usual veneer of self-consciousness." After an hour of running there comes an altered state of consciousness similar to meditation, prayer, some drug experiences, and dreaming. Emotions may well up from some untapped source and tears may come unexpectedly.[122]

Running can be part of religious rituals. In Hopi and Navajo ceremonies, young men engage in long and exhausting traditional runs. Buddhist novice monks in some monasteries in Japan also practice long-distance running. These ritual exercises may produce a deep transformation, a mystical participation with the forces of surrounding nature.

Simple labor can also bring similar spiritual encounters. Take, for example, Tolstoy's description of the ecstatic experience of his alter ego, Count Levin, in *Anna Karenina*.[123] Levin joins his serfs in mowing the estate's fields with scythes. It soon becomes apparent that Tolstoy himself had the mystical encounters he describes in the novel. He vividly shows the influence of freedom Levin feels in the wide expanses of the land, the sun beating down, the peasants joining him in an unaccustomed camaraderie. The flow of the repetitious, strenuous mowing leads to an exaltation, blocked only as "he began thinking what he was doing and trying to do it better, he was at once conscious how hard the task was, and would mow badly" (p. 272).

Tolstoy continues, in Levin's skin, to mow "and more and more often now came those moments of oblivion, when it was possible not to think of what one was doing." Tolstoy cannot leave that scene of happy memories: "…the scythe seemed to mow of itself, a body full of life and consciousness of its own, and as though by magic, without a thought being given to it, the work did itself regularly and carefully—These were the most blessed moments" (p. 273).

MOUNTAINS AND THE ECSTASY OF DANGER

Mountaineering must now be ranked among competitive sports, particularly in the drive for first ascents of great peaks around the world. Extreme exertion, hypoxia (oxygen deficiency), and danger are combined with spectacular mountain panoramas in an often-addictive chemistry. The French mountain climber Lucien Devies describes the first ascent of Annapurna:

In the extreme tension of the struggle, in the frontier of death, the universe disappears and drops away beneath us. Space, time, fear, suffering no longer exists [sic]. Everything then becomes quite simple. As on the crest of a wave or in the heart of a cyclone, we are strangely calm—not the calm of emptiness but the heart of action itself.[124]

John Muir, the great naturalist, conservationist, and founder of the Sierra Club described a difficult moment while climbing:

After gaining a point halfway to the top, I was suddenly brought to a dead stop, unable to move hand or foot either up or down. My doom appeared fixed. I must fall. There would be a moment of bewilderment, and then a lifeless rumble down the one general precipice to the glacier below. When this final danger flashed on me, I became nerve-shaken for the first time since setting foot on the mountain, and my mind seemed to fill with stifling smoke. But this terrible eclipse lasted only a moment, when life blazed forth again with preternatural clearness. I seemed suddenly to become possessed by a new sense. The other self—the ghost of by-gone experiences, Instinct, or Guardian Angel—call it what you will—came forward and assumed control. Then my trembling muscles became firm again, every rift and flaw in the rock was seen as through a microscope, and my limbs moved with a positivism with which I seemed to have nothing to do. Had I been borne aloft upon wings, my deliverance could not have been more complete.[125]

There is, in fact, a delicious edge to facing danger. Physiological reactions stir up the body; adrenaline, generated by the adrenal glands that stimulate the sympathetic nervous system, increases the heart rate, intestinal motility, perspiration, and blood pressure. The "adrenaline rush" that many people attribute to the psychological thrill of deliberately courting danger may also include an outpouring of endorphins in the brain that relieves anxiety and the fear of death.

For example, the climber Laura Waterman found herself in a life-threatening situation. She said, "Oddly enough I wasn't scared but beyond fear. Our precarious situation was so patently obvious that I felt an immense calmness and clear-headedness that comes only when you are on the thin edge between living and dying."[126]

Remarkable experiences such as this have been described again and again, in the heat of battle, and in other moments of extreme danger. A mysterious "power" appears and "takes charge," enabling the individual to cope with and sometimes overcome the predicament. This power lies as a hidden quality in most of us, although there certainly must be those who find it in their everyday lives. It is the stuff of heroism, bravery, and resourcefulness.

Ernest Hemingway obsessively captured the ritual confrontation with death of the Hispanic Toreo. He described the ultimate human drama of giving and receiving mortality: "The *faena* (the final act of the bullfight) that takes a man out of himself...that gives him an ecstasy that is, while momentary, as profound as any religious ecstasy."[127] In Hemingway's famous short story, Francis Macomber, too, shone with transcendent light after overcoming cowardice and looking death in the face, the face of a charging, wounded lion. His "short, happy life" was ecstatic after that inner, coping response, inborn but rarely used, was unleashed.

Similar to Hemingway's character, the protagonist of Stephen Crane's *The Red Badge of Courage* experienced a transformative epiphany following the violent emotions of fear and cowardice in the face of danger. As "the youth" was buffeted by the shock and awe of pitched battle, he experienced the remarkable sensory phenomenon that has been often described in this book: "Each blade of grass was bold and clear. He (the youth) thought that he was aware of every change in the thin, transparent vapor (gun smoke) that floated idly in sheets."[128] He achieved a fleeting but "sublime absence of selfishness." In modern terms it would seem that the transitory loss of ego, the subsidence of the overlay of conflicting mental conflicts, contributed to his mystical experience. This is a step toward *individuation* (a term in

Jungian psychology meaning the attainment of wholeness), as well as *kensho* (in Zen terminology the achievement of heroism, or enlightenment), and much more.[129]

A unitive transformation came to the youth after the battle, "a large sympathy for the machine of the universe," where "in the space-wide whirl of events no grain like him would be lost."[130] This spiritual dimension, a part of natural mystical experience, seems to ring true in these fictional narratives and must certainly arise from personal experience. As in all literature, truth emerges from experiential reality.

The mystical experience arising from the confrontation of danger may be the same phenomenon that illuminates the Zen meditator or the nature stalker. There are also more mundane moments of such "heroic achievements"—for example, the speaker, singer, actor, or musician beset by stage fright. Many of us have experienced a similar transformation from a trembling, sweating bowl of jelly to a confident, assertive performer. Thus we see in our daily lives psychological mechanisms in reserve that, under certain triggering conditions, help the individual overcome fear and inhibition. Indeed,

> Thus conscience does make cowards of us all
> And the native hue of resolution
> Is sicklied o'er with the pale cast of thought,
> And enterprises of great pith and moment
> With this regard their currents turn awry
> And lose the name of action.[131]

Fear is a most universal human condition, and overcoming it is heroism, ranging from small everyday confrontations to the most noble and extraordinary achievements of superhuman proportions.

In today's world, among affluent societies, extreme sports seem increasingly popular. Andrew Todhunter in *Dangerous Games* mentions ice climbing, bungee jumping, skydiving, sea kayaking in storms, and other nearly bizarre challenges to death. It seems a perversion when, "like the kendo practitioner who lays aside his wooden sword to duel with live blades, the climber—in freeing him or herself of the rope on routes where falling is synonymous with extinction—becomes a kind of mystic."[132] It may reflect on the secure, affluent society from which such participants come. They search for the "ultimate" but possibly also for that primeval hunter inside.

From all the encounters of a wide spectrum of individuals, engaged in nearly every conceivable activity from the peaceful contemplation of wild nature, of a Zen garden, a work of art or music, to the most strenuous or violent challenges, on dangerous mountains, or in deadly battle against fellow creatures, human or otherwise, there may come similar transcendent feelings. The metaphoric mountain up which these spiritual journeys ascend, through its ravines and over its ridges, culminates perhaps in a single peak, which may be called satori, individuation, bliss, nirvana, ecstasy, or any of the other expressions that describe the transformation created by a profound mystical experience. Such an experience tempers our psyche and leaves permanent memories that expand the spirit and draw us close to the unitive connection with nature.

5. The Mystic Ladder

CLIMBING THE MOUNTAIN

IN WORLD LITERATURE, the similarity of mystical experience through all lands and cultures is striking. Though the vocabulary used to conceptualize mystical experience—the subject of this chapter—varies somewhat between individuals, disciplines, and cultures, no creed or sect can alter this innate human phenomenon; the criteria appear to be universal. Hence mystical experience has been called philosophia perennis.

William James, in his great work *The Varieties of Religious Experience,* described and defined some of the feelings associated with mystical experience. He experienced his own epiphany in the Adirondacks, after a strenuous hike to the peak of Mount Marcy, at 5,344 feet the highest in New York state. As he wrote to his wife,

> The moon rose and hung above the scene before midnight, leaving only a few of the larger stars visible, and I got into a state of spiritual alertness of the most vital description. The influences of Nature...all fermented within me till it became a regular Walpurgis Night. I spent a good deal of it in the woods, where the streaming moonlight lit up things in a magical checkered play, and it seemed as if the Gods of all the nature-mythologies were holding an indescribable meeting in my breast with the moral Gods of the inner life.... It was one of the happiest lonesome nights of my

William James in 1888, seen with the caretaker Paul Ross near the barn of his new summerhouse in Chocorua, at the foot of the White Mountains in New Hampshire. He wrote in a letter to Henry James, "...75 acres of land, mountain 3500 ft. high, exquisite lake a mile long, fine oak and pine woods, valuable mineral spring, two houses and a barn, all for 900 dollars or possibly less.... The more we live the more attached we grow to the country." Sept. 17, 1886 (by permission of the Houghton Library, Harvard University).

existence, and I understand now what a poet is. He is a person who can feel the immense complexity of influences that I felt, and make some partial tracks in them for verbal statement. In point of fact I can't make a single word for all that significance, and don't know what it was significant of, so there remains, a mere boulder of impression. Doubtless in more ways than one, things in the Edinburgh lectures will be traceable to it.[133]

From that ecstasy on Mount Marcy, William James predicted its creative outcome—the monumental *Varieties of Religious Experience*, in which he gives the criteria for his term "mystical states of consciousness" as:

1. Ineffability: "The subject of it [the mystical state of mind] immediately says that it defies expression, that no adequate report of its contents can be given in words.'
2. Noetic quality: "They are states of insight into depths of truth unplumbed by the discursive intellect."
3. Transiency: "Mystical states cannot be sustained for long.... Often, when faded, their quality can be imperfectly reproduced in memory, but when they recur it is recognized, and from one occurrence to another it is susceptible of continuous development in what is felt as inner richness and importance."
4. Passivity: "...the mystic feels as if his own will were in abeyance, and indeed sometimes as if he were grasped and held by a superior power."[134]

These qualities ring true to the undercurrents I lovingly preserve from memories of spiritual adventures in nature. These feelings are, to me, *ineffable*, indescribable; *noetic*, true; *transient*, brief; and *passive*, unexpected. Let us look at them in more detail to better understand this *philosophia perennis*.

INEFFABILITY

Ineffability is characteristic of the dimension of our consciousness that cannot be expressed in words. In his *Tractatus*, Ludwig Wittgenstein wrote, "There are indeed things that cannot be put into words. They make themselves manifest. They are what is mystical."[135] We search for words to describe mystic experience, yet fail. But our words do have a role, like the shadows that suggest the shapes of objects that cannot be rendered. Intuition is the bridge that connects that shadow of the spoken word to the reality of its subject. For some, that intuition is less developed than in others. The wordlessness of the unfocused mystic and the alertness of the hunter in nature are not inarticulate. Their consciousness is fully engaged and connected. It is rather a state of mind beyond language.

Embracing the paradox of ineffability, the *Nei-yeh* (inner training of Taoism) declares that within the mind there can be an "awareness that precedes words."

> As for the Way:
> It is what the mouth cannot speak of,
> The eyes cannot see,
> And the ears cannot hear.[136]

One might say that experience is like being in neutral gear, without friction. When I try to convey that experience in words, I then must put my thinking mind into gear. My understanding of my experience is processed by the somewhat inefficient gearshift into explicit expression with a certain loss of the original tacit knowing, just as there is an energy loss through frictional heat in mechanical gears. It often seems as if one had to struggle with great difficulty through a speech impediment in order to physically express a thought. But other symbolic representation, such as parables and other metaphors, can become paths of expression to illuminate the noetic ferment surging inside. Ansel Adams saying, simply, "There are no words to convey the moods of those moments," echoes the efforts of many others where often tears replace the words. As he struggled to express his feelings for nature, Richard Jeffries wrote: "Clumsy indeed are all words the moment the wooden stage of life is left."[137] To talk or write about an experience involves reducing it to words, and as Graham Dunstan Martin asserts, "We are indeed reducing it. For it is impossible for words…to describe any natural object completely."[138]

The "transparent eye-ball" of Emerson, Goethe's *exakte sinnliche Phantasie,* the *via negativa,* the hunter's trance, all serve to connect the ineffable process of mystical experience to explicit understanding.

Noesis

James defines noetic quality (*noeo* from the Greek meaning "apprehend") as "states of insight into depths of truth unplumbed by the discursive intellect" that carry with them "a curious sense of author-ity for after-time."[139] It is unshakeable truth, intuitively apprehended, ineffable and lasting to the one experiencing it.

We know more than we know how to tell. Our consciousness is a vast dimension, little of which is in our awareness at any given moment. Knowing is part of consciousness. The philosopher Michael Polanyi suggests that there are two kinds of knowing, the tacit and the explicit. As Graham Dunstan Martin interprets them, the explicit type of knowledge is that which can be expressed in words and sym-bols, while tacit knowledge cannot.[140]

Swedenborg, in his *Arcana Coelestia*, considered that the certainty of reality, which I consider an equivalent to James's noetic quality, came from an inner voice from the Lord, flowing into the deeper parts of our thought, which could be our subconscious. He wrote that revelations from perception (which I interpret to mean the input from our senses) represented the "good and true" (which could be intuitive, noetic, or tacit knowing), while verbal revelation (discur-sive or explicit knowing), lacked true meaning.[141] We might define intuition in Swedenborg's words as "the immediate apprehension of the mind without reasoning," or we could consider it analogous to *yin*, the transcendental realm of tacit knowing.

Qi (also spelled *ch'i*) is a word from the ancient Chinese that may express the bridging of the reality of tacit knowing and the abstraction of explicit expression. It is vitality, giving the breath of life to all matter, an animistic principle. It works through nature and poetry to evoke the ineffable state of mind that lies at the heart of mystical experience.[142] *Qi* is also a way toward the core of Chinese esthetics. For example, the *qi* of a peculiarly shaped rock or oddly twisted tree trunk can evoke a transcendent feeling, not directly pleasure, but something deeper in the heart of things, at the heart of the universe perhaps. From that esthetic experience may come much of the art of Zen. Through *qi* one can reach the "endless dialectic of inner experience" that Wordsworth and others sought to express.

When I see a particular silhouette of a mountain framed by a sunset, or that cold light of Venus above the fire-red cliffs, or simply a certain pattern of leaves on the water, a feeling enters me that I know. That is an approximation in words of what *qi* represents. Those feelings are the essence of reality, the conduit to our connection with the universe. William James wrote, "...the recesses of feeling, the darker, blinder strata of character, are the only places in the world in which we catch real fact in the making."[143] Hidden deep in each of us, these "strata" are near what some may speculate is the soul. They are reachable when we clear the way by sweeping aside the bits of information, the "noise" that blocks the inner journey to the plenum of our ground state.

Henri Bergson, the French humanist philosopher much admired by William James, wrote in 1911, "In the humanity of which we are a part, intuition is, in fact, almost completely sacrificed to intellect."[144] He postulated that life originated from a supra-consciousness and that choice rather than passive and random steps in evolutionary change lay at the heart of all. That supra-consciousness, according to Bergson, inhabited a dimension beyond our rational comprehension, yet our intuition, like a ray of light, could pierce that darkness not comprehended by our intellect and reveal the unity of spirit with the universe.

Bergson included in this unity the simultaneous evolution of all life when he said, "All organized beings, from the humblest to the highest, from the first origins of life to the time in which we are, and in all places as in all times, do but evidence a single impulse, the inverse of the movement of matter, and in itself indivisible."[145]

The psychiatrist Richard Bucke expressed the noetic dimension as "cosmic consciousness." As we attune our intuition to the open-ended world as interpreted by quantum theory, it may be that James, Bucke, and other early visionaries are smiling in their graves at the radical new vision gradually unfolding: one in which our consciousness is not alone but at one with a consciousness of all life, indeed, a cosmic consciousness.

TRANSIENCE, PASSIVITY, AND OTHER CHARACTERISTICS

The other two Jamesian properties of the mystical experience are transience and passivity. The apprehension of mystical experience is swift and sure. Neurochemical mechanisms that may come from evolutionary patterns of survival ensure that the experience passes swiftly, though it is stored forever in the memory and surely changes the individual who has known it. This transience may be just as well, since most of us need to get on with mundane matters. Humanity and all other life would scarcely survive if caught up in a beatific mystical moment forever.

Passivity has two components: one is the sudden and often surprising act of mystical revelation, catching the subject unawares. Ansel Adams was "suddenly arrested" by the awareness of light. The other is that the mind is made receptive for intuition, either deliberately as in meditation or other exercise, or through the *via negativa* of the unmediated mind; the hunter, for example, expands the inner vision that allows the magical feeling to enter.

Thus mystical exaltation can enter one's being spontaneously. There is no recipe for this phenomenon, since, according to James, "Being a secret and a mystery, it often comes in mysteriously unexpected ways."[146] This was Alter's experience, and James's, too, in his magic night on Mount Marcy.

One might consider a fifth characteristic of mystical experience to be transformation. The memory of such an experience, lasting and immutable, somehow changes one forever—whether in a small way, such as an increased understanding of one's place in the world, or as a complete change of purpose, lifestyle, location, etc.

Many have suggested still other characteristics, such as the feeling of cosmic or worldly unity, an immanence that reveals to us the reality of being. Athletes have particularly noted a sense of timelessness, or a slowing of time. The extraordinary enhancement of light, called photism, seems to be fairly common and is often dramatic. And the loss of a sense of ego is part of the unitive experience, the sense of becoming one with the universe, with the One, with God-head, with nature.

Another thinker, the neurologist and Zen disciple James Austin, has staged the "ordinary and extraordinary alternate states of consciousness" on the mystic ladder into nine ascending levels, each level characterized by type and intensity of awareness, sensate perceptions, duration, sequelae, and other properties.[147]

Stage 1 defines an ordinary waking state of mundane life with no special meditative states other than occasional daydreams. Stages 2 and 3 are levels of "slow wave" and "desynchronized" sleep, or dream sleep. In the latter stage, vivid and imaginative dreams can arise during REM (rapid eye movement) episodes. Austin believes that the dream material can, on rare occasions, give a comprehensive resolving insight after awaking.

Stage 4 consists of awareness of the "suchness of things," a selfless compassion of ongoing duration. In stage 5, "epiphanies" occur in natural outdoor settings. Stage 6 includes a "vacant, blank interval of no consciousness"; stage 7 a sudden enlightenment also known as *kensho;* stage 8 is "ultimate being," a state of grace reserved "for the very few"; and finally, in stage 9, the rarest of all, consciousness leads to "true equanimity, simplicity, and stability," presumably the province of the rare saint, guru, or prophet.

FREUD AND THE "OCEANIC FEELING"

Others refer to the "oceanic feeling" in mystical experience. A theme often repeated in Hindu scriptures is the merging of the soul or the self in that great mother, the ocean. The now popular term "oceanic feeling" comes from a biography about the nineteenth-century Bengali philosopher Ramakrishna. As Romain Rolland, the French poet and philosopher, tells it, Ramakrishna once entered into a deeply disturbed psychic state and was prepared to kill himself, when suddenly:

The whole scene, doors, windows, the temple itself vanished.... It seemed as if nothing existed anymore. Instead I saw an ocean...boundless and dazzling. In whatever direction I looked great luminous waves were rising. They bore down on me with a great roar, as if to swallow me, they broke over me, they engulfed me. I lost all natural consciousness and I fell. How I passed that day and the next I know not. Round me rolled an ocean of ineffable joy. And in the depths of my being I was conscious of the presence of the Divine Mother.[148]

Rolland conveyed his thoughts about this "oceanic feeling" in his correspondence with Sigmund Freud.[149] Freud responded with a description of the chaos that this idea had stirred in his concepts of the mind.

I had sent him [Rolland] my little book, which treats religion as an illusion, and he answered that he agreed entirely with my views on religion as an illusion and he answered that he was sorry I had not properly appreciated the ultimate source of religious sentiments. This consists of a peculiar feeling, which never leaves him personally, which he finds shared by many others, and which he may suppose millions more also experience. It is a feeling which he would like to call a sensation of eternity, a feeling as of something limitless, unbounded, something "oceanic." It is, he says, a purely subjective experience, not an article of belief; it implies no assurance of personal immortality, but it is the source of the religious spirit.... These views, expressed by my friend whom I so greatly honour and who himself once in poetry described the magic of illusion, put me in a difficult position. I cannot discover this "oceanic" feeling in myself.[150]

It is interesting to note, however, that Freud had described an experience many years earlier (1895) that fits the criteria of ecstasy, certainly a feeling close to that which may be called "oceanic." He had labored every night for weeks on an attempt to describe psychoanalysis in scientific terms, with a great deal of frustration and inner turmoil. His exhaustion from this effort seriously affected his daily clinical practice. Then, one night, "tormented with just that amount of pain that seems to be the best state to make my brain function, the barriers were suddenly raised, the veils fell away, and it was possible to see through from the details of the neuroses to the determinants of consciousness. Everything seemed to fit together. The gears were in mesh...."[151] Though Freud may not have possessed or cultivated the intuition that would have allowed him to grasp Rolland's words about the oceanic feeling— it is possible, even probable, that human beings vary considerably in genetic and cultural heritage with respect to spiritual capacity—he could still discover a capacity for the ecstatic experience so many have described, both before and after his time.

Recent Concepts

Now, many years after James and Freud lived and wrote, what can modern psychology offer to help us conceptualize mystical experience?

One modern explorer of the mind, the American psychologist Abraham Maslow, was inspired by William James's 1902 Gifford Lectures to focus on a more "humanistic" approach to spirituality than was provided by many theological teachings. Maslow's "peak experience" represents the occurrence of a sudden and intense feeling of inner power, bringing a unity of body and psyche, that can lead to a heightened sense of awareness, of wonder and awe. Ansel Adams's description of the encounter on Mount Clark and E. O. Wilson's naturalist's trance in the Surinam forest closely resemble Maslow's definition.

Maslow tried to grade the quality and intensity of such experiences on a scale from "relative" to "absolute"; that is, from "quasi-mystical," where the individual is in a state of self-awareness, conscious of having a personal experience, to a fully mystical event, where a unitive feeling with the object (the loved one, the world, the cosmos) is accompanied by a sense of timelessness and spacelessness.

"Flow" is a metaphor and a title for a mental state that the psychologist Mihaly Csikszentmihalyi studied in a wide variety of persons. He describes it as a process of "total involvement with life," a source of psychic energy that focuses attention and motivates action. The potential for flow, according to Csikszentmihalyi, is innate in most of us, but is expressed most visibly by those who tend to excel in mental and motor skills. These include, for example, musicians, athletes, artists, and rock climbers. The conditions that lead to that expression may include several components: immersion in a challenging activity, becoming one with the activity, clear goals, feedback, concentration, control, loss of self-consciousness, and transformation of time.

Csikszentmihalyi distinguishes between flow, which is a controlled and cultivated experience, and mystical experience or ecstasy, which he calls "fortuitous epiphany," i.e., completely spontaneous.[152] Yet such a distinction sounds a little arbitrary. Several elements of the concept of flow—unitive feelings, loss of self-consciousness, transformation of time—seem to be present in many of the manifestations of nature and other mystical experiences. Complete absorption in an activity, be it meditating, stalking an elk, or performing surgery, can lead to mental states that one person might call flow, but another might call mystical.

"Deep play," according to the writer Diane Ackerman, includes unself-conscious engagement with our surroundings, an exalted feeling of transcendence, and a state of optimal creative capacity. "We spend our lives," she says, "in pursuit of moments that will allow these altered states to happen."[153] The concept of "deep play" may stem from the Dutch historian Johan Huizinga's name for humanity as *Homo ludens,* from the Latin *ludere,* "to play." Play, of course, is a close companion of competition and combat. Watch cubs at play, a prelude to life beyond the nurturing comfort of maternal indulgence, an embarkation for creativity. Children's remarkable affinity for wild nature can be seen as they play in the woods and meadows, the streams and ponds. Such play can yield truly ecstatic moments that stay with one forever, like the joyous memories in Wordsworth's poems (see chapter 7).

The "Breakout Principle" is a method created by the Harvard physician Herbert Benson "to activate the natural trigger that maximizes creativity, athletic performance, productivity, and personal well-being." Benson believes that the physiological, biochemical, and neurological changes that he has observed are similar in all of the six "peaks" of experience he describes: self-awareness, creativity, productivity, athleticism, rejuvenation, and finally transcendence.[154] A key element is his "relaxation response," a spectrum of physiological changes that Benson and others have shown to occur during meditation or immersion into the quiet of nature. These changes, mediated through the autonomic nervous system from centers in the area of the limbic system, include lowered blood pressure and bradycardia (slowing of the heart), just as Wilson experienced in the "naturalist's trance." Benson as well as Ackerman, Maslow, and Csiksentmihalyi avoid the terms "mysticism" and "ecstasy," perhaps for the reasons I stated earlier, namely the pejorative connotations of vagueness, occultism, and spiritualism (the belief that the spirits of the dead can communicate with the living).

"Magical consciousness" is defined by the English theologian Susan Greenwood as an "expanded awareness" that develops the power of imagination in its connection to nature spirituality. "Magical consciousness," she says, "concerns the awareness of the interrelationship of all things in the world." But she cautions that this state of mind is "primarily natural rather than supernatural or mystical." She uses the word "magic" to imply the ability to mobilize the imagination and thus, through emotion and concentration, to change or alter consciousness.[155]

As I interpret her philosophy I see much in it of the experiences that I have described that could be considered those of nature mysticism.

I find no conflict in using the word "mysticism" interchangeably with magic consciousness, the sense of mystery of what lies within our mind, not one of supernatural beings and forces.

When James attempted to construct the "mystic ladder" he termed the lower rungs "mundane." That is, by placing all experience on the same "mystic ladder," he implied that there is no sharp distinction between ordinary experience and mystical experience. I prefer to think that the continuity of these states of mind through the range of transcendental experience toward the enlightenment of intense ecstasy has more than two dimensions. It is not just a ladder but rather a mountain up which one can climb from ridges, glaciers, cols of varying degrees of difficulty, to the one point, the apex, at the very top. Thus the slopes of this mountain represent a vast area of human creative activity that borders on the surrounding plains of everyday life and thought, where just the slightest effort to climb the mountain leads to the beginnings of mystical and creative experience.

For example, when I focus upon some task, be it repairing a motor, preparing a meal, creating a work of art, writing a treatise, or performing a surgical operation, extraneous cerebral noise becomes gradually suppressed. The focus becomes sharper and the task easier and smoother, often, as has been said, "without thinking," which in fact is true. The inner self, our unconscious mind, guides us to achieve the task. A sublime feeling may accompany this creative achievement. That feeling can achieve such intensity as to be experienced as mystical. I walk along a beach, pondering prosaic matters, and glance at the sunset, or a seashell or a bird. An indescribable feeling suddenly sweeps over me. It seems to come from a vast reservoir of transformative energy waiting somewhere inside me. Thus I paint with a broad brush and freely use the term "mystical" to describe experiences that are to many ordinary. There is no sharp edge to that border, no stepping off the ladder or the mountain. The potential for an ecstatic experience is always with us, especially when we immerse ourselves in what the physicist Sir Arthur Eddington described as "...the harmony and beauty of the

face of Nature," that is "at root one with the gladness that trans-
figures the face of man."[156] The entrance into a communion with
nature is not only a source of a deep and calm pleasure but also,
according to the Tasmanian clergyman Edward Mercer in his semi-
nal *Nature Mysticism,* "a subtle and powerful agent in aiding men to
realize some of the noblest potentialities of their being."[157]

6. The Healer and Scientist

THE SPIRITUAL TRANSCENDENCE from an encounter in nature, like other mystical experience, is healing both to the psyche and to the body. Ample evidence exists from the studies of Herbert Benson and others of the quieting of the autonomic nervous system and of the release of endorphins, both processes leading to lowered blood pressure, reduced heartbeat, a feeling of calmness and tranquility. The emotional catharsis, even including tears, from a profound encounter is yet another physiological manifestation of our limbic system.

The most immediate and dramatic effect that I have experienced, one that occurs undoubtedly to countless when entering into a natural setting, is the reduction of the feelings of stress. Health is associated with nature, illness with urbanism.

Today, physicians and surgeons are rediscovering that healing of disease and wounds involves the psyche. The placebo effect (from Latin *placere,* to please) is a treatment that has benefit although it is not directly therapeutic. Herbert Benson has introduced the term "nocebo effect" to express the opposite of the placebo effect. Nocebo effects may result from the destructive influences of society or individuals, such as the preaching of hate, suspicion, race superiority, and so on. Much human illness nowadays involves psychic damage, and modern psychosomatic medicine as exemplified by Benson and his clinic brings useful holistic concepts to current teaching and practice.[158]

The basic understanding of the psyche has in Western medicine traditionally taken second place to our often-urgent need to deal with the soma. This is changing with today's pioneering advances in psychosomatic medicine and psychiatry, and the rediscovery of the advantages of traditional healing arts. The psychologist or physician may benefit from the ancient lore of native healers and employ their methods in what is now called holistic healing.

A UNIVERSAL ART OF NATURE

The art of healing is physically as well as psychically rooted in nature. Humankind has treated illness and injury for thousands of years with plants and minerals that have often yielded remarkable remedies. These substances continue to play a major role in medical therapy. Take, for example, digitalis, quinine, belladonna, and aspirin, just a few examples from a kaleidoscopic array of substances that have very specific effects on certain human diseases and more general benefits for the symptoms of suffering from disease or injury. Nowadays most of the essential ingredients of these substances are synthesized and chemically modified, but pharmaceutical research continues to explore the benefits of new and rare plants. Teams of investigators travel throughout the forests and jungles of the world to find and test promising new plant derivatives.

Of course, not all contact with the plant world is benign. Plants have developed their own defense mechanisms to ward off predators that may threaten the ultimate goals of propagation and dissemination. There are both internal and external toxic substances. Some of these substances have been identified to be effective in destroying disease-causing predators of human beings. Many antibiotics and anti-cancer drugs from the plant world have been identified and put into use. Undoubtedly many more remain to be discovered.

Plants have become humanity's allies in protecting us from the scourges of malaria and other infestations, in relieving pain and suffering through plant-derived narcotics, and as tonics for failing organs. The ancient and modern healer and shaman both need to know the beneficial effects of plants. But modern physicians are losing contact with the ancient botanical pharmacopeia because of the demands of scientific learning and advanced technology that go under the guise of "modern medicine." This has led to the large counter-movement of "alternative" medicine, caused in part by the frustration of instinctive needs to come closer to the mystical healing powers provided by nature and transmitted by healers and shamans.

In any city one finds stores full of "natural" remedies and nutritional supplements, not always as natural as expected because of adulteration and shoddy standards. There are newsletters, circulars, and directories for naturopaths, ayurvedic practitioners, spiritualists, practitioners of Reiki, and so on, largely spawned by a widespread distrust of so-called academic or organized medicine. This distrust may drive patients to the care of natural healers who may provide psychological comfort but not effective treatment for the disease. This seems particularly true when people get cancer, which strikes fear into most minds.

During my years of practice in San Diego there came a steady stream of patients from Mexico—Americans and others who had sought the care of shady practitioners who touted effective treatments with quack remedies for often-advanced cancers. Finding the treatments ineffective, and with their condition worsening, they desperately sought the nearest help. By this time, for many, it was far too late to give effective treatment.

The credo of the great Canadian physician Sir William Osler has always guided me in my practice: "To cure sometimes, to relieve often, to comfort always." In cancer practice it is the last phrase of this aphorism that demands the most skill and spiritual energy, and I learned from my patients who came from Mexico that Western medicine was failing them in this respect. There is mystical strength in traditional healing arts, deeply connected to the Earth, that can be integrated with Western methods and rise to meet this need.

Encounter with a Traditional Healer

It is not surprising that the experiences of many healers, ancient and modern, in their search for the relief of pain and illness, have led them to transcendent mental states. This is a part of shaman- ism (from saman, "to know," in the Siberian Tungas language, or "to practice austerity" from ancient Amerindian roots), an ancient tradition wherein the shaman reaches into his or her deeply hidden psyche to convey to others the inner vision of enlightenment and the very practical powers of healing of illness.[159] The shaman is rooted in the natural world, which brings a mystical strength derived from this primeval connection. In today's Western society such an individual may be a teacher, priest, or physician.

I recall a patient that I was treating. She was a village woman, poor, barefoot, but erect and proud, dressed in her best sari and bearing wrist, arm, and ankle bracelets. Her problem was a difficult one, an advanced inoperable sarcoma invading the pelvis. She was in great pain. I was initially unsure and indecisive about how to help her. But she emanated an aura of deep calm, great awareness, and profound inner strength. Somehow a magical transfer of energy occurred, this time from patient to healer, that enabled me to for- mulate an effective treatment program that eventually gave her the needed comfort and relief from pain. I later came to know that she was the healer of her small village, a shaman with great visionary power. That power that she often transmitted to her patients, she in turn transmitted to me, a healer who was in a sense healed through a mystic process.

Many years ago a friend in Madras, a flutist, broke a bone in his hand. He was a famous virtuoso of Carnatic music and this injury represented a potential disaster for him and for the musical commu- nity of South India. Although medical specialists, skilled in ortho- pedic surgery, were available in and near the city, my friend chose to go to a traditional healer. This man, renowned as a healer of bone fractures, lived in a small, remote village. I could do little to argue the

merits of "Western" medicine and finally agreed to drive my friend
and a supporting retinue to the village.

Once there he was received in a small hut where the healer, clad
only in a dhoti and with the marks of the healer's caste drawn on his
forehead, examined him. He disdained to glance at the accompany-
ing x-ray, and forthwith set the break without benefit of anesthesia
or premedication. My friend winced from the pain but received support and sympathy from his entourage. There followed a fascinating
scene in which the healer and his assistants, in the flickering light of
oil lamps, assembled a variety of herbal pastes, plant fibers, and leaves
to immobilize the fracture site. The scene evoked for me images of
possibly similar scenes going back eons, of early humankind, skilled
with tools, slowly learning the powers of his natural ally, the plant
world, in healing disease and injury.[160]

The path of the healer, from the realm of nature to the care of
fellow humanity, persists in an ever-diminishing number of societies. Many of the traditions are worth upholding and reviving in the
technologically advanced bastions of modern medicine. There is
an evolutionary continuity that should not be broken; rather, the
modern physician and surgeon should honor those roots of the
healing tradition and allow themselves to feel the mystical connection between practitioner and patient that is the psychic core of the
healing process.

WISDOM AND HEALING

I have known fellow medical students and colleagues who seemed to
have inherited the mantle of spiritual wisdom early in life. The calling of medicine seemed to be entirely natural to them as they flow-
ered as sages and wise healers. I looked upon them with respect and
some envy. The calling of a healer is not easy to follow, and for most
of us in the helping professions, I am sure, it demands a long and
strenuous education and practical experience. However, after years

of struggle to master facts, concepts and techniques, the moment does come, I believe, to most physicians, when they can communicate directly with their patient past all the confusing terminology of technology, through their own emotional cobwebs and the anxieties of the patient. That moment, if and when it comes, signals the shamanistic moment of truth. It is an ecstasy; one stands beside oneself. A connection has been established to an altered consciousness during the process of healing. It is, in fact, a form of flow according to Mihaly Csikszentmihalyi (the psychologist and proponent of "flow" as a creative experience), but also a mystical experience in which the healer loses the sense of self and becomes unified with the patient and with the process of extirpating or correcting the illness.

Csikszentmihalyi cites interviews with surgeons who described this phenomenon in their practice. In many respects these experiences resemble those that have been called mystical. There was a feeling of "transcendence," a loss of awareness of self, and a distorted sense of time so that the clock no longer served as an "analog" of experience. Like boulderers, surgeons lose ego feeling and become united with their manipulation. They share the "beauty and power of a harmonious transpersonal system."[161]

I, too, recall similar occasions in the operating theater, itself resembling a temple of silence and devotion, when I lost the awareness of time, of stimuli extraneous to the procedure, and became strangely connected to the patient. This was particularly the case during my service in a hospital in South India, where it was the custom for the surgical team to utter a short prayer before beginning the operation. The hallowed atmosphere was powerfully conducive to attaining a mystical state. It has often been observed how conscious patients will endure painful surgery with equanimity when induced into possibly transcendent states. For example, surgery under acupuncture in China appears to resemble an induced mystical state in the patient.

Shamanism offers the holistic worldview that bridges the vast distance between modern science and our inherited intuitive wisdom of nature. That intuitive wisdom is a part of biophilia and lies at the root of the direction humanity needs to take in order to avoid human and ecological meltdown. As the psychiatrist Roger Walsh states, "We are engaged in a race between consciousness and catastrophe, and the outcome is uncertain."[162]

THE HEALER'S TRANCE

In a way similar to that of the shaman, the modern healer enters a trancelike meditation in the process of healing. I am sure this state of mind will be familiar to many if they stop to think about it. It represents a mindset that focuses—de-focuses, rather—upon a given problem, say the diagnosis of an illness.

The clinical history, the physical examination, and the laboratory data are entered into my psyche. I look again at the patient and slip into a sort of reverie, yes, trance. This helps block out extraneous "noise"—the next staff meeting, the location of my car keys, the plans for the week.

The residents look askance at me. Am I "with it"? But with time they, too, enter into the mood and a vibrant creative communication, unspoken at first, can develop between us and often with the patient. I snap to attentiveness and the magic process of thinking, feeling, and intuiting ferments to reach a hopefully beneficial solution.

This healer's trance or shamanic meditation must come from deep psychic roots whereby the direct perception of the patient's illness or injury is transmitted through engrams, the established neural circuits, of association into the memory. This process, whether it is called parallelism or creative imagination, associates that experience of perception with intuitive processes. From this comes, hopefully, a solution, mental or manipulative, to the patient's problem. As in other meditative states, *apophasis*, the emptying out of the mind, may facilitate the creative process of the healer.

This process is not unique to me: I have seen it in mentors and have learned much from this almost sacred ritual of patient rounds and bedside teaching. It is repeated, too, in the operating room, where the ritual is experienced, often silently, through the deft coordination of surgical movements, akin to the mystic dimension of coordination in bouldering (see chapter 3). I have never seen a shaman at work, but surmise that in this mystical connection we are not all that different. And the analogy can be expanded widely to a multitude of occupations, trades and other activities.

BRIDGING THE GAP

One of Einstein's widely quoted aphorisms begins, "The most beautiful and most profound emotion we can experience is the sensation of the mystical. It is the sower [more likely, source] of all true science."[163] This statement reverberates sympathetically with what I try to describe—a rational mysticism, grounded upon the intellectual understanding of our heritage, the rejection of the supernatural, and an appreciation of the vast, yet largely untapped, span of our consciousness.[164]

It is interesting, however, that when Einstein originally made this statement in 1931 he did not mention "the mystical," but rather "the mysterious." Though he is said to have changed the statement later, in his youth it seems he bristled at the term "mysticism," possibly because of the positivist and materialistic outlook prevalent among scientists in the late nineteenth century.[165]

This reflects the widely held pejorative perception that I discussed in the introduction, of mysticism as a vague and cloudy quasi-religion associated with occultism, telekinesis, and the supernatural. In later life, it appears that Einstein acknowledged that the term "mysticism" suggested what he was trying to convey as the "most beautiful and most profound emotion" that we can feel. This highly creative man spoke and wrote about his belief in "cosmic religious experience" as "the strongest and noblest mainspring of scientific research." He ultimately, therefore, equates his personal belief, his "cosmic religion," with mystical experience.[166]

Healing is a science and an art, a rational and a mystical process, and a logical place to bridge the gap of perception between the rationality of science and nature mysticism. Both concern the relationship of humanity with nature; both need to come closer together in humankind's thinking in order to increase the understanding and true love of our coexistence with all life. But how can we form that bridge, the unified worldview that truly values the spirit in science?

As Einstein did eventually, the Danish theoretical physicist Niels Bohr rejected the common understanding of mysticism as a form of fuzzy religious belief, a semantic problem. In his correspondence with Werner Heisenberg in 1925, he wrote, "I am at the present, with all my power, pushing myself to enter into the mysticism of nature."[167] (Heisenberg himself, at the moment of creating and confirming the mathematical proofs for the astonishing theory of quantum mechanics, in the middle of the night on the island of Helgoland, experienced an epiphany sitting on a high rock looking out upon the ocean as dawn came. He described the giddy sensation of seeing "into the heart of nature" in an interview with the physicists Paul Buckley and David Peat.[168]) From this statement and others, we can believe that Bohr, like many others particularly in the field of theoretical physics, did believe in a rational mysticism as a pathway toward the apprehension of reality. This term embodies the rapid disappearance in the postmodern era of the superficially perceived dichotomy between science and spirituality.

This is a positive trend, for the human mind's ability to grasp transcendent understanding may often be diminished by the pervasive forces of scientific materialism. The Harvard biologist Richard Lewontin, a close colleague of the late Stephen Jay Gould, swung down a verbal cleaver between science and mysticism when he criticized such ideas as sociobiology, evolutionary psychology, and cultural evolution, stating that they "disarm us in our struggle to maintain science against mysticism."[169] Other scientists, such as David Bohm, Brian Josephson, Fritjof Capra, and John Eccles are questioning this mindset that denies a window into ultimate reality. E. O. Wilson writes that mystical union is truly part of the human spirit, and is a vital subject for investigation and understanding by mystics and scientists alike.[170] I may add that mystics and scientists are often one and the same—and I sense that Wilson is one such thinker.

We seem now to be in a transitional epoch in which, as in the Chinese proverb quoted by Capra in *The Tao of Physics,* mystics understand the roots of Tao but not the branches, while scientists understand the branches but not the roots. These separate world-views may be merging, as the noetic dimension, perhaps long considered not just mystical but also vague and dreamy, now seems ever closer to concepts of the New Physics. The worlds of biological, psychic, and quantum evolution are merging into a unifying dimension that is difficult for me to grasp yet appears firmly rooted in experimental science.

The Sufi philosopher Pir Vilayat Inayat Khan emphasizes the experiential nature that unites science and mysticism, declaring, "What the scientist and the mystic have most in common is the importance they attach to experience.... Science has learned through experience to eschew dogma, and it is this very principle that is at the heart of the distinction between religion and spirituality."[171] Indeed, empirical observations and reflections upon personal experience and their effects upon our thinking and emotions are at the heart of my thesis.

Sir Arthur Eddington's "pointer readings" (of measuring instruments) are now dominating modern neurobiology. The plotting of electrochemical and metabolic activity in the brain during mystical/religious experiences is providing a vast new array of information. Yet scholars such as Eugene Taylor, a Harvard teacher and an authority on William James, are concerned about the facile correlation of neurological measurements with religious experiences. Taylor declares, "Neurology can tell us no more about the reality of religious experience, or any other form of experience, than its mechanics." In other words, Taylor maintains that human experience, particularly religious experience, is of necessity beyond scientific interpretation.

This is not necessarily true, as is illustrated by James Austin's approach to the neurological basis of mystic experience (see chapter 4). As a neurologist he painstakingly correlates neurological information with the experiences of Zen practices, particularly meditation. Bertrand Russell wrote, "Even the cautious and patient investigation of truth by science...may be fostered and nourished by the very spirit of reverence in which mysticism lives and moves."[172]

The neuroscientists Eugene d'Aquili and Andrew Newberg query:

> Is spiritual experience nothing more than a neurological construct created by and within the brain, or does a state of absolute union (with the universe) that the mystics describe in fact exist and the mind has developed the capacity to perceive it? Science offers no clear way to resolve the question.[173]

I reply that it may not matter as long as the experience is real and potentially transforming of one's worldview, behavior, and the love that comes with such transcendent moments. However, by trying to fathom the underlying mechanisms and conditions that lead to such experience, we gain knowledge that lets us see more clearly, without superstition, our place in the universe. Scientific knowledge can be a road to follow when guided by mystic consciousness, and there need be no conflict between the scientific and the mystical connection with nature.

7. The Psychobiology of Mystical Experience

"With all your science can you tell how it is, and whence it is, that light comes into the soul?"

HENRY THOREAU, *Journal*

"Reductionism is a way to understand complexity."

E. O. WILSON, *Consilience*

MYSTICAL MODELS

THE ROOTS OF those feelings that we consider to be spiritual or mystical appear to grow from the depths of our consciousness. Beginning with models that served as metaphors for mystical experience, thinkers have repeatedly turned to developing scientific disciplines for the tools to dig ever deeper to reach this frontier of our psyche.

James considered mystical experience to be the "mother sea and fountain-head" of all religions, and to inhabit a region deeper than that of intellect. This region was, to James, an "extended subliminal self with a thin partition through which messages make irruption." Not knowing the farther margins of that subliminal field of consciousness, James evoked the existence beyond of an "Absolute mind" or a "distinct deity."[174]

James presented with openness and candor four of his own patently mystical experiences, which were "sudden and incomprehensible enlargements of the conscious field, bring[ing] with them a curious sense of cognition of real fact."[175] It is of interest that William James wrote this essay in 1910, eight years following the Gifford Lectures in Edinburgh. He remarked, "Whether my treatment of mystical states will shed more light or darkness, I do not know, for my own constitution shuts me out from their enjoyment almost entirely, and I can speak of them only at second hand."[176]

In a letter to his close friend Henry Rankin following the Edinburgh lectures, James wrote:

> I think that the fixed point in me is the conviction that our "rational" consciousness touches but a portion of the real universe and that our life is fed by the "mystical" region as well. I have no mystical experience of my own, but just enough of the germ of mysticism in me to recognize the region from which their voice comes when I hear it.[177]

In this he was strongly influenced by the now obscure German physician and physicist Gustav Theodore Fechner (1801–1887), considered a founder of experimental psychology. Fechner received a medical degree at the University of Leipzig but then proceeded to study physics and mathematics. In a wide-ranging career he became professor of physics, and later philosophy, at the same institution. He was a towering presence in the nineteenth century and an inspiration to, among others, Sigmund Freud. He formulated the basic law of psychology that states that the intensity of sensation increases as the logarithm of the stimulus, called the Fechner-Weber law. His mantle was assumed by his student Wilhelm Wundt (1832–1920), who attracted numerous future leaders in psychology to his laboratory, including William James.

James at first had mixed feelings about Fechner. He called much of Fechner's psychophysics "moonshiny" and elsewhere refers to the "patent whimsy" of "such a dear old man."[178] Yet he took seriously much of Fechner's panpsychic writing and returned again and again to the oceanic metaphors surrounding Fechner's wave theory of consciousness. He carefully read Fechner's now largely forgotten (and untranslated) thoughts on cosmic consciousness and saw in his words the glimmerings of the idea of consciousness as an evolutionary phenomenon, leading back to an ultimate collective dimension in the universe. Indeed, well before the new concept of Gaia, James viewed the Earth as a sentient organism. He agreed with Fechner's "great analogy" of the relationship of the senses to the minds, not only of humanity, but also with every living thing.[179]

James viewed Fechner in a new light after the Gifford Lectures. He has this to say in *Pluralistic Universe* in 1909:

> The original sin, according to Fechner, of both our popular and scientific thinking, is our inveterate habit of regarding the spiritual not as the rule but as an exception in the midst of nature. Instead of believing our life to be fed at the breasts of the greater life, our individuality to be sustained by the greater individuality, which must necessarily have more consciousness and more independence than all that it brings forth, we habitually treat whatever lies outside of our life as so much slag and ashes of life only; or if we believe in the Divine Spirit, we fancy him on the one side as bodiless and nature as soulless on the other. What comfort or peace, asks Fechner, can come from such a doctrine? The flowers wither at its breath, the stars turn to stone; our own body grows unworthy of our spirit and sinks into a tenement of carnal senses only. The book of nature turns into a volume on mechanics, in which whatever has life is treated as a sort of anomaly; a great chasm of separation yawns between us and all that is higher than ourselves, and God becomes a nest of thin abstractions.[180]

James considered Fechner's wave theory to be a major step toward the understanding of consciousness.[181] Fechner conceived a diagrammatic representation of "waking consciousness" in the shape of a wave, its crest extending above a horizontal limit that he called the threshold. He then postulated a number of "wavelets" that represented various states of consciousness. The moment and amplitude

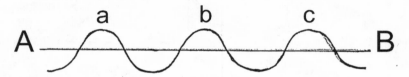

Fechner's wave-scheme of consciousness. Line AB represents the threshold above which the wave pattern (a, b, c) integrates consciousness, while below this threshold lie the fields of unconsciousness (Unbewusstein). *From* Elemente der Psychophysik, *530.*

of these "wavelets" are variable, as shown in his original diagram (see above).[182] They resemble the pattern of the alpha sine wave of "resting" consciousness discovered much later by the technique of electroencephalography. The threshold according to Fechner's theory could vary in height and separated consciousness (above) from subconsciousness (below).

After translating and studying Fechner's concepts,[183] William James developed the metaphor of an oceanic tide, its water surface being the threshold. The tidal ebb uncovers a vast area of shoreline that is, in other words, the usually hidden subconscious area of our psyche.[184]

James suggests that mystical intuition may be a sudden, large extension of "waking" consciousness, so that knowledge that is ordinarily what he calls transmarginal (i.e., subliminal) may become perceived like land exposed "on an unusually flat shore at the ebb of the spring tide," an apt New England metaphor. James then describes his own experience of a sudden widening of the conscious field (as the tide or threshold falls): "The larger panorama perceived fills the mind with exhilaration and sense of mental power."[185] In his field of consciousness, he distinguishes sensation, which can be termed effortful consciousness, from the vast reservoir of memories, concepts, and "conational" states that generally lies below the tidal surface. This reservoir when suddenly brought into view gives the conditions for "a kind of consciousness in all essential respects like that termed mystical." He invokes his criteria of mystical states by indicating that these experiences are transient (since the changing level of threshold is transient) and there is a sense of reality (noesis) as well as enlargement, illumination, and unification. The experiences are intuitive and perceptual rather than conceptual, since the field of consciousness exposed to view does not attract attention to individual objects but rather gives a feeling of "tremendous muchness suddenly revealed."

Michael Polanyi's distinction between tacit and explicit knowing appears to me to suggest yet another dimension to the Jamesian model of consciousness, where both types of knowing occupy certain spaces in our waking consciousness. The important functions of learning, recognition, and sensation—in fact, all experience—are primarily tacit, of which only a tiny bit can be made explicit. Although James Joyce tried in his novels, his words represent an iota of the tip of the mountain projecting above the clouds, below which exists a gigantic mass of unknown dimensions.

The dimensions of the region of subliminal consciousness are unknown even to the most advanced students of neurobiology. William James's British contemporary Frederick W. Myers, and his French colleague Pierre Janet, who described *desaggregation,* the dissociation of levels of consciousness, excited James's interest in the source of the "vast sea" of memory and thought that lies within us in ever-deeper layers, perhaps down to ancient inherited engrams that correspond in part to Jung's concept of archetype.

James's colleague and friend, the American philosopher Charles Saunders Peirce, postulated another metaphorical image of consciousness when he said,

> I think of consciousness as a bottomless lake, whose waters seem transparent, yet into which we can clearly see but a little way. But in this water there are countless objects at different depths; and certain influences will give certain kinds of these objects an upward influence which may be intense enough and continue long enough to bring them into the upward visible layer. After the impulse ceases they commence to sink downwards.[186]

In these poetic and imaginative metaphors there is a common thread: consciousness is a continuum through visible layers (waking consciousness) into ever-deeper layers (subliminal, subconscious, unconscious) to an unknown, perhaps infinite ground. Alternatively, in a recent popular book on consciousness, the American psychiatrist Allan Hobson visualizes consciousness as a sphere, resembling a toy balloon, floating in a space with coordinates of apparently scientifically derived parameters. It resembles a Cartesian diver, at the surface in waking consciousness and deeply submerged during sleep. But the models of James, Peirce, Myers, and Janet seem intuitively to better express the unfathomable dimensions of consciousness.

It may be useful to try to connect the theoretical and metaphorical concepts of Fechner and James with modern ideas about consciousness. It has been generally believed that consciousness is the functional product of different areas of the brain, often referred to as modules or subsystems, and that there is no single "seat of consciousness."[187] New advances in neurophysiological research show that there is a persistent wave of electrical activity at a periodicity of about 40 Hz (cycles per second) that "sweeps regularly from below the forehead to behind the nape of the neck" and orchestrates consciousness from separate centers in the brain.[188] Fechner, decades before modern neurophysiology, seems to have anticipated the existence of a wave pattern involved in consciousness.

Quantum theory places consciousness into a "nonphysical dimension" where the signals between brain synapses are connected in a quantum mechanical continuity. With newer techniques of brain function measurement there may be evidence that 40 Hz neural oscillations "are the most likely neural basis for consciousness itself...[and] are the neural basis for...unitive intelligence [possibly mystic experience]."[189] Theorists of quantum mechanics suggest that "revelatory" experiences may raise brain activity from 10^8 to some 10^{12} bits per second.[190]

In other words, according to this theory, a mystical experience involves (as James suggested) a vast expansion of brain activity (or consciousness), recalling the oceanic metaphor and giving credence to Fechner's wave theory.

In 1880, in his discussion on consciousness in *Principles,* William James created a model for the chapter on "The Stream of Thought."[191] He assumed a connection of memory to all conscious moments, an "ocean" underlying all awareness. This reservoir of memory is vastly larger than any instantaneous conscious state, yet it is somehow connected. He constructed a prescient solution, a diagrammatic representation of a sentence that demonstrated his concept of the stream of thought. James described and explained this model in very practical terms:

> If we make a solid wood frame with the sentence written on its front, and the time scale on one of its sides, if we spread flatly a sheet of India rubber over its top, on which rectangular coordinates are painted, and slide a smooth ball under the rubber in the direction of 0 to "yesterday," the bulging of the membrane along this diagonal at successive moments will symbolize the changing of the thought's content in a way plain enough, after what has been said, to call for no more explanation. Or to express it in cerebral terms, it will show the relative intensities, at successive moments, of the several nerve-processes to which the various parts of the thought object correspond.[192] (see following page)

The three axes represented time, intensity, and content. The representation of a stream of thought resembled a Gaussian wave rising from a flat substrate that represented subconsciousness. The instantaneous conscious state changed with every moment of time.[193]

The physicist David Bohm depicts a similar diagrammatic representation of thought and consciousness. He visualizes thought and memory as a ripple upon a stream of consciousness that itself flows in a vast ocean of the ground state.[194] The attribute common to both James's and Bohm's ideas is movement, the dynamic process of thought that can scarcely be captured in a static image. I have

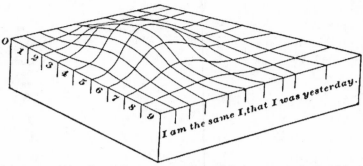

The stream of thought. William James constructed this topographic model of his concept of the stream of consciousness. One axis (x) represents, according to James, "the objects or contents of (the) thought"; the second axis (y) indicates "relative intensities...of the several neural-processes to which the various parts of the thought-object correspond"; and the third axis (z) represents time, "a finite length of thought's stream." From The Principles of Psychology, *vol. 1, 180.*

constructed a model that is based upon those of William James and David Bohm, but designed to depict the threshold (*limin*), the "flimsy curtain" separating the moving wave of "waking" consciousness from the "vast sea" of subliminal consciousness. The lowering or dissipation of this threshold can lead to the "sudden enhancement of consciousness" that James associated with mystical experience.[195] Although utterly simplistic, the model (facing page) may also provide an easier understanding of the mystic experience and its connection with creativity.

ALTERED STATES OF CONSCIOUSNESS

Taking another approach, can mystical experience be explained by the chemical and electrical reactions of neuronal connections? Aldous Huxley, always bold in statement, said:

> In one way or another, all our experiences are chemically con-
> ditioned, and if we imagine that some are purely "spiritual,"
> purely "intellectual," purely "aesthetic," it is merely because
> we have never troubled to investigate the internal chemical

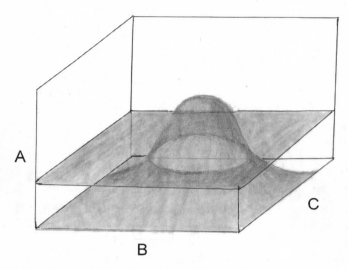

William James's stream of thought model revised. Axis A represents intensity, Axis B represents content, and Axis C represents time. The horizontal plane is the threshold, separating "waking" consciousness from subconscious states.

environment at the moment of their occurrence. Furthermore, it is a matter of historical record that most contemplatives worked systematically to modify their body chemistry, with a view to creating the internal conditions favorable to spiritual insight. When they are not starving themselves into low blood sugar and vitamin deficiency, they were beating themselves into intoxication with histamine, adrenaline, and decomposed protein in uncomfortable positions in order to create the psychophysical symptoms of stress. In the intervals they sang interminable songs, thus increasing the carbon dioxide in the lungs and the blood stream, or, if they were Orientals, they did breathing exercises to accomplish the same purpose.[196]

This was a preamble to his argument for seeking mystical experience in a much easier way, through drugs. Huxley anticipated much that we now know scientifically of some of the preconditions for achieving such states. Yet mental and physiological stress is by no means the only path. Herbert Benson's "relaxation response" follows the tranquil and passive practice of meditation or the immersion in the quietness of nature. The physiological changes of meditation and spontaneous moments of mystical experience, including decreased oxygen consumption, heart and respiratory rates, and blood pressure, have also been found in experiments in cats on the stimulation of the hypothalamus and are considered by Benson to be an adaptive reaction protecting the body from overstress.[197]

Huxley claimed to have experienced all the transports of ecstasy by ingesting the plant extract mescaline and recommended its use in the everyday services of the Christian Church. His chief critic in these extravagant and, to many, outrageous claims was the Oxford orientologist Robert Zaehner, who had this to say:

> At the impressionable age of twenty I was in fact the subject of a "mystical" experience, which combined all the principal traits described in *The Doors of Perception*. When Mr. Huxley speaks of being a "Not-self in the Not-self which is a chair," I knew that, as far as the normal, rational consciousness is concerned, he is talking horrid gibberish, but I equally knew that I have myself experienced precisely this and the joy experienced as a result of this uncontrollable and inexplicable expansion of the personality is not to be brushed aside as a mere illusion. On the contrary: beside it the ordinary world of sense experience seems pathetically unreal. This occurred to me when I was an undergraduate and before I became interested in Oriental languages: it came wholly unheralded and no stimulants of any kind were involved.[198]

How do we reconcile these views? First, it is obvious that our inner neurophysiological environment is affected in both phenomena, one artificially induced, the other naturally induced. What can neurological science clarify?

The brash but often perceptive Huxley may have been right, at least in part. As we have seen, there are physiologically stressful components to many of the mystical encounters related earlier.

Steven Alter had just finished a strenuous trek, Peter Matthiessen bivouacked, exhausted, during a frightening storm, and Leo Tolstoy (in the person of Levin) sweated in the repetitive mowing of wheat. But countless others have experienced similar moments of transcendence in physical states of peace and calm. Is there a common thread joining these two extremes?

Some neurophysiological insights into these and other spiritual events can be gleaned from a recent comprehensive review by a group of European psychologists of the current knowledge about altered states of consciousness (ASC).[199] Though mystical experience is referred to mostly indirectly, we can begin to hypothesize about the science of mystical states from the information given on near-death experience, meditation, sensory deprivation, and relaxation response techniques.

Near-death experience (NDE) is, of course, an episode generally involving extreme stress that can lead to a number of remembered perceptions including peacefulness, out-of-body experience, dark tunnel experience, photism, hearing of music, slowing of time, and speeding of thought. Naturally NDE cannot be reproduced experimentally, but experiments inducing conditions of extreme hypoxia can reproduce some of the features of NDE. According to the investigators, cerebral hypoxia (low oxygen levels in the brain) may be a principal consequence of near-terminal life events that can deplete neurotransmitter reserves in the limbic system, leading to auditory and visual hallucinations but also feelings of peace and calm.

Enhancements or distortions of light and color are frequent in ecstatic experiences.[200] Saul, later the Apostle Paul, on his fateful journey to Damascus encountered a "blinding light, stronger than the sun" which event lead to his conversion to be a disciple of Jesus (Acts 22:6). Ansel Adams, too, experienced a "pointed awareness of light," and the young Wordsworth was transported when "An auxiliary light/Came to my mind which on the setting sun/Bestowed new splendor...."[201] Nietzsche, in a moment of creative ecstasy, described in *Ecce Homo* the perception of "a superabundance of light."

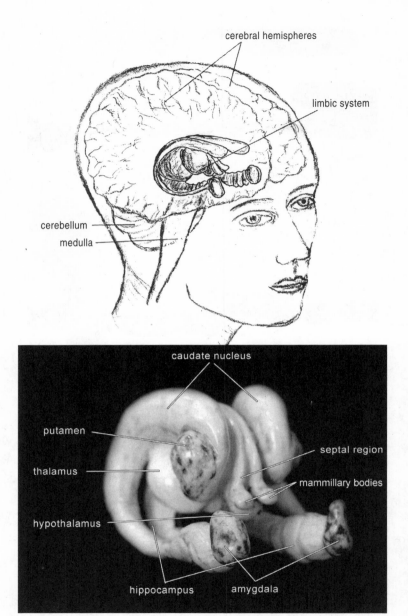

The human brain and its "limbic" system, flanked by the basal ganglia. The main divisions of the brain are shown. At the base of the forebrain are a number of complex, quaintly named and oddly shaped structures, which form a sort of coordinated or "limbic" system that has been referred to in the past as the visceral brain. They include the sea-horse (hippocampus), the almonds (amygdala), the lower room (hypothalamus) and other smaller components.

Bill Wilson, the founder of Alcoholics Anonymous, describes a striking example of photism. He had been struggling with depression and alcoholism for years and was at the edge of a spiritual abyss. He was in a state of "complete, absolute surrender" when,

> Suddenly, my room blazed with an indescribably white light. I was seized with an ecstasy beyond description. Every joy I had known was pale by comparison. The light—I was conscious of nothing else for a time.... I know not how long I remained in that state, but finally the light and the ecstasy subsided.... As I became quieter, a great peace stole over me, and this was accompanied by a sensation difficult to describe. I became acutely conscious of a Presence, which seemed like a veritable sea of living spirit. I lay on the shores of a new world.

Bill Wilson never took another drink and went on to found AA.[202]

The psychiatrist Stanley Dean, describing what he calls the "ultra-conscious summit," quotes from Whitman's *Leaves of Grass*—"Light rare, untellable, lighting the very light—beyond all scopes, descriptions, languages"—and from Dante's *Divine Comedy*: "The light I saw was like a blazing river... / Fixing my gaze upon the Eternal Light/ I saw within its depths, / Bound up with love together in one volume, /The scattered leaves of all the universe."[203]

This association of visual phenomena with ecstatic experiences may relate to a second path of visual perception in the brain (see facing image for other anatomical references in this chapter) that is modulated through the superior colliculus of the thalamus, and which Gordon Taylor has called "thalamic vision." It is conceivable that as a surge of enkephalins blocks incoming impulses to the midbrain, the visual cortex signals are reduced and the more primitive visual pathway predominates, resulting in the various perceptions of light and color that have been described.[204] This second visual system, according to Austin, may have appeared early in evolution.[205] It is more developed in primitive monkeys than in modern primates. The signals from the retina go directly to the superior colliculi, through the pulvinar of the thalamus and finally to the cerebral cortex. There may be an evolutionary advantage in that the signals are processed in the midbrain. In other words, no thinking is necessary for a reflex avoidance of danger.

Photism has also been called "the white light experience" and "light-of-the-void."[206] The psychologist Harry Hunt suggests that meditation may allow the visual field to be more accessible to direct experience. Thus visual perception can be enhanced in meditative and other mystic states. Meditation may involve deliberate breathing exercises that can result in varying blood pH levels (acidity and alkalinity) due to the depletion or increased levels of carbon dioxide. These changes have been said to lead to perceptions of tranquility, unitive feelings, etc., but the precise neurophysiological mechanisms are still unknown.[207]

Perhaps closer to a psychobiological explanation of mystical experience are data that come from studies of sensory deprivation. Indeed, trancelike states and other "quiet" moments of ecstatic revelation may follow the deliberate or spontaneous cutting off of sensory information.

Such experiments have been performed on subjects who volunteer to be in conditions of total absence of sensory input, such as in total darkness and in floatation tanks at body temperature, etc. The results of the sensory deprivation experiments included reduction of blood epinephrine levels and increase of beta-endorphin levels (an enkephalin mediating certain centers in the limbic system and the pretemporal part of the cerebral cortex). These, among other changes, may lead to the observed improvements in memory performance, decreased anxiety, increase of vigor, curiosity and creativity, as determined by various psychological tests following sensory deprivation experiments. One group of scientists has gone so far as to try to block certain areas of the brain in the belief, based on observation of autistic patients, that "savant-like" abilities may emerge when incoming cerebral signals are interrupted. A method called transcranial magnetic stimulation has been reported to temporarily enhance creative abilities in a small number of volunteer subjects.[208]

In both meditation and sensory deprivation experiments, and in the decreased sympathetic nervous system activity of Benson's relaxation response, an increased activity of limbic neurotransmitters may occur. According to the UCSD psychiatry professor Arnold Mandell, such activity leads to a decrease of serotonin regulation of the limbic structures, thus releasing or "disinhibiting" effectual and cognitive processes characteristic of a state of "transcendental consciousness."[209] It has also been discovered that opioid receptor sites are concentrated in the limbic system and the closely connected frontal lobes of the cerebrum.[210] These findings indicate further that much of what we associate with the feelings of spirituality, of mystical experience, and of emotions are associated with the limbic system and the closely connected prefrontal cerebral cortex.

The pharmacologist Avram Goldstein studied the "thrill" experienced by students listening to music. He was able to block that "thrill" in a significant number of test subjects by administering naloxone, a blocker of opiate action. This suggests, as the psychologist Charles Levinthal recounts it, that even the ecstasy of hearing music is mediated, at least in part, by the release of endorphin peptides.[211]

A major effect of these chemical signals may be deafferentation (a cutoff of incoming information). If a structure is subjected to deafferentation it may fire according to its own "inner logic."[212] For example, Arnold Mandell contends that certain cells in the hippocampus initiate the mental events resulting in ecstasy. The hippocampus, among its other functions, integrates two neurological circuits: one is the external information flow, which may be referred to as the "external circuit"; the other receives relevant subjective information from other parts of the brain and is called the "internal circuit." Following stress or other stimuli the external circuit may be blocked by enkephalins and the internal circuit is amplified so that it becomes the only source of information. When the external circuit is blocked "there arises an experience of peace, calm and even ecstasy."

As the studies of Benson have shown, this feeling of tranquility following a mystical experience results in a physiological state often manifested by reduced rates of breathing and heartbeat. This may be caused by an autonomic neural response, mediated through the centers of the brain, particularly in the limbic system, from actions of neurotransmitters such as dopamine and the endorphins.

In psychological terms, according to the Jungian psychologist Manisha Roy, this closure of the external and enhancement of the internal circuit may lead in the individual to an overwhelming aware-ness of the Self, following submission of the ego, leading to feelings of cosmic unity that can be called mystical experience.[213]

OHM'S LAW ANALOGY

Our waking consciousness is normally filled with millions of "bits" of information: What appointments do I have today? Who was that girl I saw last night? Where are my socks? All these are enough to daily fill a book or more by James Joyce. It is these bits of information that Taoist mystical practice aims to clear out in the process called *apophasis*—the emptying out of mundane consciousness[214]—in order to reach the Way, *Tao,* the unitive experience leading to wisdom. It is "sweeping out the mind" to reach inner power, *Te.*[215] Many religious mystics from other traditions (such as Swedenborg) thought that disciples should empty their souls to become vessels to receive the divinity of revelation. Whatever your chosen discipline or inspiration, wiping out that data allows one to have a sort of cerebral vacuum; in other words, one loses an internal blockage or resistance that, in physical terms, can be measured electrically as ohms.

Ohm's Law of electricity states that resistance (R) is inversely proportional to current (A); where V is voltage or potential, $R = V/A$. Experience tells both the hunter and the meditator that an enhanced perception comes during moments of trance: the sky is brighter; the focus is sharper; the thoughts that eventually flood back are remarkably deeper, and energy, fortitude, and endurance are greater. All these represent the flow of current into our psyche. In other words, as our psychic resistance, a product of mental clutter and superfluous information, diminishes, the flow of psychic current increases.

We can stretch this analogy further when we look at the physical phenomenon of superconductivity. Normally a current of electrons flowing through a conducting material such as metal meets a resistance that, according to Ohm's Law, impedes the current flow. By cooling the conductor sufficiently to stop the vibrating atoms in the lattice of the structure of the conducting material, one can achieve a state where resistance drops to nearly zero and the flow of current is no longer impeded. As resistance nears zero, the flow of current can approach infinity.

In the analogy, mental resistance can be "cooled" sufficiently by quenching the neural circuits carrying our burden of mundane psychic "noise" that impedes the internal flow of thought between the hippocampus and cerebrum. In this way mental superconductivity, if it exists, can produce superconsciousness, an untrammeled flow of internal neural impulses that can lead to extraordinary enlightenment and creativity. Indeed, the core of mystical experience may be pure consciousness, emptied of sensory and cognitive content.

Another analogy for the mystical apophasis or void of being might be a concept of quantum theory called the "quantum vacuum." As David Peat describes it, the condition for achieving a perfect vacuum is to empty a space completely of energy. This is a ground state of pure cosmic emptiness. Yet, according to quantum mechanics theory, within "incredibly tiny intervals of time" particles can flow in and out of that space, exchange identities, and create a huge amount of energy, to the absolutely incredible point where "...the energy within a cubic centimeter of the vacuum state would vastly exceed the energy content of the universe."[216] Consciousness, too, can be considered "empty," with no shape or form, yet containing incredible mental processes. The theologian Robert Forman terms consciousness as "empty plenitude."[217] Most religions contain some concept of apophasis, such as the *via negativa, sunyata,* and the Clear Light of the Void. The so-called vacuum–plenum paradox was introduced by the psychologist W. T. Stace to try to understand how such states of mind can achieve the near-limitless revelations we associate with profound mystical experience.[218] This paradox by analogy is, according to quantum physics, no paradox where Peat described how pure emptiness can contain a nearly infinite amount of energy. The simplistic model stemming from Ohm's Law demonstrates this analogy in down-to-earth terms when it shows the potential within each of us.

Into that vacuum of apophasis can come the energy of love, meaning a union that gives a state of freedom, unshackled from the bonds of hate, prejudice, and ignorance. Swedenborg called this *proprium,* a state of owning one's soul.[219]

"NEUROTHEOLOGY"

Beginning with Mandell's pioneering monograph, *Toward a Psychobiology of Transcendence: God in the Brain,* presented in 1978, a discipline called "neurotheology" has been growing. Other titles, based primarily on recent discoveries in neurobiology and neuropharmacology, include *Religion in the Mind, Why God Won't Go Away,* and *The Mystical Mind: Probing the Biology of Religious Experience.* In essence they argue that the perception of God arises in our brain.

Modern diagnostic techniques such as PET (photon emission tomography) and SPECT (single photon emission computed tomography) can detect real-time changes in the brain's metabolism during various mental stimuli exercises by following the changes of blood flow in various parts of the brain. These dynamic studies plus our new knowledge of neurochemistry permits certain conclusions about the sites of the brain involved in meditative exercises, and in other conditions that can be termed mystical or religiously ecstatic.

The SPECT studies by neuroscientists Eugene D'Aquili and Anthony Newberg of individuals in active meditation indicate that the prefrontal cortical area of the cerebrum has increased blood flow, evidently related to increased neural activity, while, simultaneously, the portion of parietal cerebral cortex known as the orientation association area has decreased blood flow. This suggests to the authors that, while sensory input is blocked, the internal circuit relating the prefrontal cortex to the limbic system operates in the possibly "reverberating" mode suggested by Mandell that may evoke "ecstatic and blissful" feelings.[220]

Newberg and D'Aquili believe that mystical experience can also occur when both the sympathetic and parasympathetic neurohumoral systems are subjected to high levels of prolonged and intense physical activity such as the prolonged concentration or repetitive motion seen in running or mountain climbing.

But these brain scans are still relatively crude ways of measuring the incredibly detailed complexity of the mind. They merely reflect changes in blood flow, an indirect indicator of neural activity. I wonder what a brain scan of Ansel Adams would show, on that memorable morning climbing Mount Clark, or of Saul on the road to Damascus.

Another question has recently entered the neurotheology arena. Is the perception of God inherited? Is the ability to have a deeply religious or spiritual experience handed down in our genes? Population surveys, some which have been cited in this book, show that thirty to fifty percent of surveyed individuals have recognized such experiences in themselves. If these studies predict that between one-third and one-half of individuals are "spiritual," why then are the others not? Is it because of the presence or absence of an inherited trait, or is it because of the presence or absence of cultural conditioning?

Take for example the topic of this book, nature mysticism. William James, among others, states, "Certain aspects of nature seem to have a peculiar power of awakening...mystical moods." Most of the "striking cases" that James collected to illustrate his chapter on mysticism in *Varieties of Religious Experience* came from "out of doors."[221] Is it possible, therefore, that as the world population continues its move into urban communities, approaching soon two-thirds of all humanity, it will experience further alienation from our natural world and from opportunities for spiritual experience? Or that when the places of worship and the religious traditions within families disappear (as they did in Russia in Soviet times and are doing as well in many "advanced" cultures), the religious experience of the affected population and its descendents can wither away? How much of the tendency toward religious practice is "nature" and how much is "nurture"?

One investigator, the NIH geneticist Dean Hamer, claims to show that it is nature in at least two-thirds of individuals in a particular study. In his book *The God Gene: How Faith Is Hardwired into Our Genes,* Hamer explores the origins of spiritual experience.[222] But there are few facts to support his title.

Supposedly there is at least one gene that is associated with spirituality that was determined through a "self-transcendence scale" in a questionnaire given to 1,001 college student volunteers. This "God gene" is one that codes for a monoamine transporter, a protein that controls certain neurotransmitters, "the same brain chemicals that can be triggered by certain drugs that can bring about mystical experience" (p. 11).

Although forty-seven percent of the subjects were identified to be in a "higher spirituality" group, there are no figures to demonstrate how Hamer associates this group with a higher preponderance of one particular gene. Further, the question of a causal relationship would have to be answered. Much remains to be done.

Drugs and Mystic Experience

Whether or not it is appropriate to attempt to explain the root of religious feeling by a diagram of electrical and chemical circuits in our brain, there is a connection to a disturbing and worldwide problem of immense importance—drug-induced ecstasy. An understanding of the neural mechanisms of mystical experience may someday lead to better ways of coping with the global epidemic of substance abuse.

We know that humankind has used drugs since the earliest times to induce transcendental feeling. Poppies, mushrooms, cacti, cocoa leaves, betel nut, cannabis, tobacco, and other plants, plus alcohol, have all been used in religious rites and as a source of "recreation." The road from use to abuse and addiction follows a vision of paradise, e.g., an ecstatic experience, after ingestion of something that can be grown, extracted, brewed, and bought. It leads, however, down a steepening slope toward a point of no return. My main guide, William James, himself experimented with "laughing gas," nitrous oxide, and induced in himself a form of ecstasy:

> Nitrous oxide and ether, especially nitrous oxide, when sufficiently diluted with air, stimulate the mystical consciousness in an extraordinary degree. Depth beyond depth of truth seems revealed to the inhaler. This truth fades out, however, or escapes, at the moment of coming to; and if any words remain over in which it seemed to clothe itself, they prove to be the veriest nonsense. Nevertheless, the sense of a profound meaning having been there persists; and I know more than one person who is persuaded that in the nitrous oxide trance we have genuine metaphysical revelation.

> Some years ago I myself made some observations on this aspect of nitrous oxide intoxication, and reported them in print. One conclusion was forced on my mind at that time, and my impression of its truth has ever since remained unshaken. It

is that our waking consciousness, rational consciousness as we call it, is but one special type of consciousness, whilst all about it, parted from it by the filmiest of screens, there lie potential forms of consciousness entirely different. We may go through life without suspecting their existence; but apply the requisite stimulus, and at a touch they are there in all their completeness, definite types of mentality that probably somewhere have their field of application and adaptation. No account of the universe in its totality can be final which leaves these other forms of consciousness quite disregarded.[223]

This remarkable experience, reported by a courageous and honest scientist, psychologist and philosopher, was followed by the claims of numerous experimenters of psychedelic drugs, in recent years notably by Aldous Huxley and Timothy Leary. The latter, an enthusiastic proselytizer for the benefits of LSD (lysergic acid diethylamide), stirred a whole generation with his slogan "tune in, turn on, and drop out." While today his words seem to me largely meaningless, his conclusions empty,[224] James's experimental approach seems bold and pioneering, just as it was when he first wrote about these questions that lie at the heart of our search for meaning.[225]

Although Huxley and Leary believed drug experiences could be equated with ecstasy, there are many who disagree. William James put his finger on this point when, following his own nitrous-oxide-induced experience, he exclaimed, "The truth fades out...and if any words remain over...they prove to be the veriest nonsense." Jiddhu Krishnamurti, an early leader of the Theosophical movement, asked, "What is the necessity of taking drugs at all—drugs that promise a psychedelic expansion of the mind, great visions and intensity? Apparently one takes them because one's own perceptions are dull. Clarity is dimmed and one's life is rather shallow, mediocre, and meaningless; one takes them to go beyond mediocrity." Mystical experience in nature, or the hunter's trance, can create the clarity that Krishnamurti says is lacking in many people's perception and in the transcendence that is often missing in their lives.

The Zen Buddhists, such as the Abbot Zenkei Shibayama, also declare their disapproval: "Recently there have been people who talk about instant enlightenment, or those who take drugs in an attempt to experience *satori* (enlightenment). Whatever claims they make, I declare that such approaches are not authentic true Zen at all."[226]

From my own limited experience, I would not wish to alter the circumstances, the unforgettable moments, and the feelings of certainty of the few ecstasies most of us are likely to have. The English writer Marghanita Laski estimates that the average number of ecstasies experienced by normal individuals in a lifetime is six. The capacity to experience them diminishes with age, reflecting the diminution of neurotransmitters in the course of aging.[227] Naturally induced ecstasy, often unexpected and thus more precious in its delight, is a revelation of the inner self. As a scientist, however, I seek to explain it in familiar terms, in our language of critical reason. I can visualize the process as one of circuits relating to the inner self, to the managing ego and to incoming signals from the external world. Feedback loops serve to stabilize and equilibrate, yet certain conditions can lead to a dampening of the external circuit, allowing me to know my innermost being momentarily; other signals then automatically quench that moment of self-awareness, as if to say, "That is enough for now." Thus our own natural homeostatic mechanisms that balance us physically and mentally are normally in charge and help to preserve our integrity. Because this may not occur for drug-induced ecstasy, users are at risk for drug dependence and addiction.[228]

An article in the *New York Times,* printed July 26,1998, reports:

The National Institute of Drug Abuse estimates that there are four million drug addicts in the United States, two million to three million that are hooked on cocaine. Another 800,000 are heroin addicts. Our Government will spend $3.2 billion in

1998 to treat addicts. Other costs, for prevention, drug-related crime and lost productivity, total more than $60 billion a year. Dr. Alan Leshner, director of the institute, believes chemical methods of prevention appear promising.

"We have come to understand how every drug of abuse works in the brain," he states. "We've identified receptors in the brain and cloned them. We know the circuits that they activate and we know some of the common elements that may relate to addiction."

Dr. George Bigelow, psychiatrist at Johns Hopkins, says that much recent research has focused on the neurotransmitter dopamine. Many drugs of abuse, including cocaine, amphetamine, opiates, marijuana, and nicotine, act on the dopamine system in the midbrain. Bigelow thinks that there is a potential problem with drugs that target the dopamine system. "It might be the final common pathway for all kinds of rewarding things, food, sex, and the joys of music and art," he says. "So it's probably not a pathway we want to eliminate. We need to find a way to block cocaine and let people enjoy other rewards." Even then it may not take care of the cravings that former users feel, often many years after they have quit.

It now appears that a "reward circuitry" operates via a dopamine pathway from the ventral tegmental area just above the hippocampus to the nucleus accumbens, in front of the amygdala and deep beneath the frontal cortex. The amygdala are involved in assessing the degree of pleasure and sending signals to the hippocampus, which fixes the memories of that experience.[229]

"One thing that makes addiction so difficult is that there is a big learning basis, and we don't have any way of making it go away," Dr. Bigelow says. "People learn to get high by using drugs, and they never forget the experience. It's a burden that addicts carry for life. To me," he adds, "that's one of the strongest arguments for prevention, and for avoiding even experimental use, because you risk having experiences that you don't forget and that continue to control and manipulate you in ways you do not want."

Why do people turn to drugs in increasing numbers in America and much of the so-called developed world? Many have argued that every human being is born with an innate drive to experience altered states of consciousness periodically. Some equate this drive with the instinct for religious experience. It is possible therefore that the attenuation of religious and spiritual feeling in our present era leaves a vacuum for this innate need. Indeed, religious conversion, among other activities such as meditation and intense absorption in creative processes, has been a frequent solution for reformed addicts.

I believe the ultimate solution lies in prevention. This may seem impossible in today's world—yet I hope that through education, both secular and religious, more people can come to know the incredibly rich resource of ecstatic experience that is available to all, uncovering a new dimensions in one's life, and making artificial methods unnecessary.

Michael Ziegler, a rabbi and psychologist, writes about psychedelic religious experiences and urges that humanity today is in need of "powerful medicines" that can reawaken the creative capacity to find new ways to live, with ourselves, with others, and with the planet.[230] Certainly. But Rabbi Ziegler refers to entheogens, drugs that induce mystical experience, and their "sacred use" in the postmodern era. Is humanity so weak and undeveloped that it must rely on such crutches to achieve the mystical state of mind? Ziegler's statement is cogent, but the "powerful medicine" for me is a big dose of renewal of our sacred bond with nature.

The neurochemical basis for mystic states is unquestionably far more complicated than what modern neurosciences have explored to date. Peripheral scanning techniques offer perhaps only a hint as to the underlying mechanisms and pathways. Yet to be explained is the revelation of mystical experience arising from conditions of total absence of stress or respiratory modulation. Though the neurochemical pathways can be traced that transmit and receive the emotional feelings of mystical experience, reductionism has its limits in delineating the transcendence of that experience. There is something that still lies beyond scientific understanding: that is our spirit.

We do not know what consciousness is. We are struggling in a dark cave, like our Paleolithic ancestors, to depict something that we feel more than we know. Models such as those discussed in this chapter can be looked upon as some sort of tool or handhold encountered in the darkness. For another kind of guide, we can turn to the work of the poet and the artist.

8. The Poet and Artist

But what is it that sits in my heart,
That breathes so quietly, and without lungs—
That is here, here in this world, and yet not here?
MARY OLIVER, Riprap

In the world's audience hall, the simple blade of grass sits on
The same carpet with the sunbeam and the stars of
    midnight.
Thus my songs share their seats in the heart of the world
    with
The music of the clouds and forests.
RABINDRANATH TAGORE, The Gardener

POETRY AND NATURE

IN A WAY, poets are mystics: they attempt to put into words feelings that are difficult or impossible to express in everyday prose. These feelings extend beyond the bounds of the spoken or written word, beyond the range of the "discursive intellect." It may be poetic metaphor that approaches most clearly the expression of transcendent states of consciousness. In essence, the syntax of poetry seeks to express the implicit, as do music and visual art.

The poetic response to nature is intertwined with the human response, just as on that ecstatic night on Mount Marcy that William

James described later in a letter to his wife, declaring, "I now know what a poet is. He is a person who can feel the immense complexity of influences that I felt, and make some partial tracks in them for verbal statement."

The poet tries to strip the outer foliage of everyday life to reveal the bare structure of what nourishes our inner selves, without which we spiritually die. To increase our understanding of ourselves in this tiny biosphere shared with our relatives—every cell of every microorganism, plant, or animal—in this vast incomprehensible space of the universe—that is the proper task of the nature poet, the literary artist translating primal truths into words. For example, he or she can invest the spirit of nature with a liberating symbolism, with metaphor, rhyme, and rhythm that brings us closer to the true reality of being.

Nature's various moods can evoke profound stirrings in the acute observer, who then becomes a spiritual participant in the dialogue. The poet Kathleen Raine calls nature the house of the soul. The nature poet, in an "endless dialectic of inner experience," seeks, not outer knowledge, but knowledge of being, through a dialogue between the outer and the inner, the explicit and the tacit.[231] The "knowledge of being" is the revelation that nature brings to poetry through the spiritual harmony of the poet's perceptions.

In recognizing the beneficence of a spirit that pervades all being, Wallace Stevens beautifully expressed and reconciled the distinction for the poet between theocratic and natural or pantheistic religion:

> An old argument with me is that the true religious force in the world is not in the church but the world itself: the mysterious callings of Nature and our responses. What incessant murmurs fill that ever-laboring, tireless church! But today in my walk I thought that after all there is no conflict of forces but rather a contrast. In the cathedral I felt one presence; on the highway I felt another. Two different deities presented themselves; and, though I have only cloudy visions of either, yet I feel the

distinction between them. The priest in me worshipped one God at one shrine; the poet another God at another shrine.... As I sat dreaming with the Congregation I felt how the glittering altar worked on my senses stimulating and consoling them; and as I went tramping through the fields and woods I beheld every leaf and blade of grass revealing or betokening the Invisible.[232]

SUBLIMITY AND DELIGHTFUL HORROR

In the eighteenth century there emerged a new appreciation of nature as a source of beauty and emotion. The essayist Edmund Burke, using terminology that strikes many today as quaint and awkward, wrote, "The passion caused by the great and sublime in nature...is Astonishment; and astonishment is that state of the soul, in which all its motions are suspended, with some degree of horror." He added, "The sublime...anticipates our reasonings, and hurries us on by an irresistible force."[233]

In another section of his *Philosophical Enquiry into the Origin of Our Ideas of the Sublime and Beautiful,* he commented, "Infinity has a tendency to fill the mind with the sort of delightful horror, which is the most genuine effect, and truest test of the sublime."[234]

Correct interpretation of these statements requires knowledge of the contemporary meanings and usages of words such as "astonishment," "sublime," and "horror." For example, Burke used the term "sublime" more in the context of a feeling, something inward, than as a descriptive term. Consider, too, that these expressions come from Latin or Greek roots, with which all literati of that era were conversant.

The Latin root of the word *astonishment* (*tonare,* to thunder) connotes surprise from a natural event of large impact. It is a word suggesting the passivity that William James associated with mystical experience.

Sublime, from the Latin *sublimes,* derived from *sub-, under,* and *limen, threshold,* or *lintel,* has a less clear derivation. The *OED* considers *sub-* in this instance to mean "up to," not "under." Yet nowhere is this supported in the various definitions of the prefix. The "sublime" generally refers to the highest regions of thought, affecting the mind with a sense of overwhelming grandeur or irresistible power, deep reverence or lofty emotion. But might an eighteenth-century classicist have considered the sublime state of mind as existing in a vast, uncharted sea of subconsciousness, under the threshold of consciousness? Certainly the term *subliminal* carries this meaning today.

Finally, the word *horror* and its derivatives are today readily associated with terror, loathsomeness, and shock. But the Latin root, *horrere,* means to bristle or shudder, and in the eighteenth century could refer to ruggedness, as in nature, that caused a shudder or a thrill. Indeed, the phrase "delightful horror" immediately suggests the idea of a frisson, the emotional thrill of a beautiful and transcending experience.

Wordsworth and his contemporaries used such words in their poetry of nature experience. The Romantic era brought back humanity's feeling of connection with its natural roots. Where the growing forces of urbanization and industrialization tended to see nature as an alien and often threatening power, the naturalists, poets, and scientists assimilated the spirit of the biosphere into their thinking and emotions. That love and understanding of nature lives on today, but is being displaced by the overwhelming forces of industrialization and global consumer economies that threaten our biosphere and our survival.

WORDSWORTH AS A NATURE MYSTIC

Wordsworth's prose and poetry are pervaded by the theme of the writer's connection to the environment. His panpsychism (the feeling that all matter is living, thus conscious) surely arose from his childhood memories, such as the ones described below in *The Pre-lude* (book one):

> Was it for this
> That one, the fairest of all rivers, loved
> To blend his murmurs with my nurse's song,
> And from his alder shades and rocky falls,
> And from his fords and shallows, sent a voice
> That flowed along my dreams? For this, didst thou,
> O Derwent! Winding among grassy holms
> Where I was looking on, a babe in arms,
> Make ceaseless music that composed my thoughts
> To more than infant softness, giving me
> Amid the fretful buildings of mankind
> A foretaste. A dim earnest, of the calm
> That Nature breathes among the hills and groves.
>
> (lines 271–285)

The river has nourished the poet as his nurse of nature. The "fretful buildings of mankind" become chastened by the power of his connection through the River Derwent to the primal sources of his, and our, ultimate birth.

His feelings become more ecstatic and primitive as the image of the river continues, and a truly erotic union with Mother Nature ensues:

> Oh, many a time have I, a five years' child,
> In a small mill-race severed from the stream,
> Made one long bathing of a summer's day;
> Basked in the sun, and plunged and basked again
> Alternate, all a summer's day, or scoured
> The sandy fields, leaping through flowery groves
> Of yellow ragwort; or, when rock and hill,
> The woods, and distant Skiddaw's lofty height,
> Were bronzed with deep radiance, stood alone
> Beneath the sky, as if I were born

On Indian plains, and from my mother's hut
Had run abroad in wantonness, to sport
A naked savage, in the thunder shower.

(lines 291–304)

Ancient pagan rituals, particularly among northern European tribes, involved wild dances of naked ecstasy in the sun-warmed forests of midsummer. To this day, many "civilized" individuals feel the need to divest themselves of clothes in attempting to more closely connect with nature—which in Scandinavia at least is a perfectly accepted form of midsummer behavior.

In his way, Wordsworth helped to turn theology back toward a spiritual religion. He celebrated the primitive forces that had in ancient times, through ignorant fear and awe, formed pagan worship[235]:

For I have learned
To look on nature, not as in the hour
Of thoughtless youth; but hearing oftentimes
The still sad music of humanity,
Nor harsh nor grating, though of ample power
To chasten and subdue. And I have felt a presence
That disturbs me with joy of elevated thoughts; a sense
    sublime
Of something more deeply interfused,
Whose dwelling is the light of setting suns,
And the round ocean and living air,
And the blue sky, and the mind of man:
A motion and a spirit, that impels
All thinking things, all objects of thought,
And rolls through all things. Therefore am I still
A lover of meadows and woods,
And mountains; and of all the mighty world
Of eye, and ear,—both what they half create,
And what perceive; well pleased to recognize
In nature and the language of the sense,

The anchor of purest thoughts, the nurse,
The guide, the guardian of my heart, and soul
Of all my moral being.

(lines 88–111)

Wordsworth revived, in simple language often strange to the ears of eighteenth-century English literati, the reverence for nature that had lain largely dormant during centuries of Christian theology.

His prescient intuition of what we now know from cosmology and evolutionary biology enhances the impact of his timeless ode to nature. Quantum energy is "deeply interfused" in "the light of setting suns." The "round ocean" and "living air" are truly living. The dynamic homeostatic changes in these media, part of our biosphere, were certainly not known in Wordsworth's day. The "motion and spirit" of "all thinking things" suggest all of life, not only the minds of human beings. Julian Huxley was deeply impressed by these lines, and after he formulated his concept of evolutionary humanism he was able to connect Wordsworth's words with more recent scientific thought.[236]

Wordsworth was among the first to be called a "nature poet," and the "mystical germ" was surely in him. He is not, however, without critics. Aldous Huxley asserted that:

The Wordsworthian adoration of Nature has two principal defects. The first is that it is only possible where Nature has been nearly or quite enslaved by man. The second is that it is only possible for those who are prepared to falsify their immediate intuitions of Nature.... Our direct intuitions of Nature tell us that the world is bottomlessly strange: alien, even when it is kind and beautiful, sometimes even unimaginably, because inhumanly, evil.

There is much to criticize in that statement. It is almost incomprehensible in this postmodern time to accept the anthropocentric idea of nature, in any manifestation, as being evil or even alien. Our scientific understanding of the forces that operate in this universe permits us to accept the impassivity of destiny. Consequently love is possible for even an unenslaved nature. The "Wordsworthian adoration" was his true intuition of Nature, be it slave or wild.

Huxley proceeds to lambaste the poet: "A voyage through the tropics would have cured him (Wordsworth) of his too easy and comfortable pantheism."[237] Poor Wordsworth! He had only his bucolic, rural eighteenth-century England as inspiration (beside the obligatory tours to the Continent). Perhaps he, as most other Europeans of that era, would have been overcome by tropical heat and lushness. We are all, however, more or less, captives of our native environment, accustomed to our own climate and geography. Perhaps there are or have been Asian, African, or Siberian poets equivalent to Wordsworth who would be dismayed by the rainy and foggy English countryside!

In addition to Huxley, there are others who have criticized or satirized the sometimes overblown and laudatory paeans to nature that became popular in the Romantic era, particularly the nineteenth century. It is well perhaps to balance excessive feelings that may arise from strong emotions evoked by any object. The writer Joyce Carol Oates, in amusement, writes, "It (Nature) inspires a painfully limited set of responses from 'nature-writers'—REVERENCE, AWE, PIETY, MYSTICAL ONENESS." She goes on seriously, however, to raise issue with the anthropocentricism, the "Nature-adoration," the "Nature-as-(moral)-instruction for mankind" of some of the genres of nature writing.

The dilettantism of some nature writing, it seems to me, is a valid criticism by Oates. It is easy to bask in the glory of a sunset, in the majesty of snow-clad peaks, and the splendor of whatever you will. But I believe nature writing transcends romanticism and is addressing the heart of the question of humanity's relationship with the environment, the need for respect of "nature as it is," a living, breathing presence, a being to which we owe our existence. Wordsworth, in this context, was more than a romantic poet.

Others, such as the oriental scholar Robert Zaehner and the psychiatrist Richard Bucke, have questioned Wordsworth's mystical antecedents. Zaehner called it likely that "to judge from his writings, he does not seem to have had a 'unitive' experience." I offer in answer to this an incident recorded by Wordsworth's friend Thomas De Quincey, in which the poet experienced and described such a phenomenon. In Wordsworth's words:

> I have remarked, from my earliest days, that if, under any circumstances, the attention is energetically braced up to an act of steady observation, or of steady expectation, then, if this intense condition of vigilance should suddenly relax, at that moment any beautiful, any impressively visual object, or collection of objects, falling upon the eye, is carried to the heart with a power not known under other circumstances.

> Just now, my ear was placed upon the stretch, in order to catch any sound of wheels that might come down upon the Lake of Wythburn from the Keswick road; at the very instant when I raised my head from the ground, in final abandonment of hope for this night, at the very instant when the organs of attention were all once relaxing from their tension, the bright star hanging in the air above those outlines of massy blackness, fell suddenly upon my eye, and penetrated my capacity of apprehension with a pathos and a sense of the Infinite, that would not have arrested me under other circumstances.[238]

The poet had spontaneously found a mystical moment and had recognized the experience. The circumstances are strikingly similar to Zen techniques of receptive meditation and to the transcendental experience of the hunter's trance. The glittering, bright star then appeared to trigger the full ecstatic moment, like the piercing cold light of Venus over the New Mexico mountains (chapter 1).

Wordsworth's mystical view of nature can also be viewed in the light of the writings of the eighteenth-century German mystic Jacob Boehm.[239] The interpretation of esthetic values in Boehm's worldview shows that the poet sees beauty as created by our natural world; that there is no other basis for esthetic creation. Wordsworth's "wise passiveness" is a "peaceful and detached reverie" that freed him from mundane concerns and enabled the fringes and depths of consciousness to become manifest.[240]

The intuitions that Wordsworth experienced on his walks along the rivers and into the hills evolved eventually into moral convictions. His reflections about nature are not as emotive regarding their sentient aspects as they are regarding their mystic significance. He perceived and expressed that the spirit of nature (for he undoubtedly believed that nature, animate and inanimate, was living) communicated with humanity, thus enabling us to grasp the certainty of an absolute union with nature.

And how well did the poet succeed in conveying the spirit of his Muse to an audience in a comprehensible way? The English poet and philosopher Frederic William Henry Myers (1842–1901)—the same who introduced the term "subliminal consciousness" and strongly influenced William James's thinking in this area—put the following conditions to poetic understanding:

> The communion with Nature, which is capable of being at times sublimed to an incommunicable ecstasy, must be capable also of explaining Nature to us so far as she can be explained; there must be *axiomata media* (middle truth) of natural religion; there must be something in the poetic truths standing midway between mystic intuition and delicate observation.[241]

Indeed, the task is to bridge the tacit and the explicit; and this I believe Wordsworth did.

The practices of Taoism and Zen would have suited this English poet. That distance between the tacit and explicit spanned an understanding of discovery, made by many over the centuries, of the calm and centering that comes from the spiritual union with nature. "The meanest flower that blows," he wrote, contains "thoughts too deep for tears." He felt that humanity's interest was to receive nature's blessings and not to impose its own caprices, as evocatively expressed in *The Prelude*: "I know that Nature never did betray the heart that loved her."

HENRY THOREAU

> If with closed ears and eyes I consult consciousness for a moment—Immediately are all walls and barriers dissipated— earth rolls from under me, and I float, by the impetus derived from the earth and the system—a subjective-heavily laden thought, in the midst of an unknown and infinite sea, or else and swell like a vast ocean of though—without rock or head- land. Where are all riddles solved, all straight lines making their two ends to meet —eternity and space gamboling famil- iarly through my depths? I am a restful kernel in the magazine of the universe. (Thoreau, *Journal*)[242]

Henry David Thoreau is little recognized as a poet, yet much that he wrote about nature is poetic. In addition to the lines that are delib- erately conceived as verse—often stilted to our ears—his prose in *Walden* and other books, and particularly in his journals, is laced through and through with the free and spontaneous qualities of poetic expression. This expression is that of nature mysticism—the spiritual bond with the primeval Mother Earth.

This strange, solitary, yet all-too-human man broke through the constraints of nineteenth-century convention to become among the first to awaken the American spirit to honor its deep connection with its natural roots. While much of American society was focused on the "conquering" of the land (and its original inhabitants), voices such as Thoreau's rang out, indeed growing louder with each succeeding generation—one day hopefully to reach the numbers needed to make a significant turn away from ecological disaster.

The New England transcendentalists were rebels, questioning the precepts of their contemporary church and society. At the heart of their philosophy lay the lessons learned from intuition, from direct experience. They believed one's destiny was determined largely by individual choice. Emerson's "great nature" was the vessel of all being, the source of a universal soul, apprehended by the subconscious state. And the evolution of humanity contained its own fall from grace. "Man is a dwarf of himself," according to Emerson, "for he was once filled with the spirit of nature but shrank from what he was and could be."[243] Nature mysticism was surely close to the ideals of the Transcendentalist movement.

Thoreau, for example, embraced "wildness" and drew it into his self. He perceived the world as a means and a symbol, and presented himself, to the admiration of Emerson, as a transcendentalist of simplicity and roughness.[244] His spiritual unity with nature went beyond physical proximity. It was when nature presented a mystical mirror of himself that Thoreau created, particularly in his early years, the poetic writings that are recorded in his private journal. Those words were unfettered by the need to publish in the accepted style of the time. In one entry he described the function of the poet:

> He must be more than natural—even supernatural. Nature
> will not speak through but along with him. His voice will not
> proceed from her midst, but, breathing on her, will make her
> the expression of his thought. He then poeticizes when he takes
> a fact out of nature into spirit. He speaks without reference
> to time or place. His thought is one world, hers another, He
> is another Nature,—Nature's brother. Kindly offices do they
> perform for one another. Each publishes the other's truth.[245]

But Thoreau the poet could voice the elegiac song, which he briefly reveals in the often lyrical *A Week on the Concord and Merrimack Rivers.*

But now there comes unsought, unseen,
Some clear, divine electuary,
And I who had but sensual been,
Grow sensible, and as God is, am wary.

I hearing get who had but ears,
And sight, who had but eyes before,
I moments lived who lived but years,
And truth discern who knew but learning's lore.

I hear beyond the range of sound,
I see beyond the range of sight,
New earths and skies and seas around,
And in my day the sun doth pale his light.

A clear and ancient harmony
Pierces my soul through all its din,
As through its utmost melody,—
Farther behind than they—farther within.

More swift its bolt than lightning is,
Its voice than thunder is more loud,
It doth expand my privacies
To all, and leave me single in the crowd.

It speaks with such authority,
With so serene and lofty tone,
That idle Time runs gadding by,
And leaves me with eternity alone.

Then chiefly is my natal hour,
And only then my prime of life,
Of manhood's strength it is the flower,
'Tis peace's end and war's beginning strife.[246]

Following Thoreau and the other Transcendental poets of New England, among whom I count Emily Dickinson as well as Walt Whitman and Herman Melville, generations of American poets have carried on the traditions of extolling the human connection with nature. The mystical connection, too, is part of this poetry. In *Imagining the Earth: Poetry and the Vision of Nature*, John Elder selects the writings of Robinson Jeffers, Gary Snyder, Annie Dillard, Peter Matthiessen, A. R. Ammons, and Robert Bly, and comments, "Through their attentiveness, expansiveness, and strategies for reaching beyond what they have learned to say, America's poets of nature, too [referring also to Wordsworth] surprise us into imagining the Earth."[247]

Among modern American poets, perhaps Annie Dillard most exemplifies Thoreau's legacy. Like Thoreau, much of her poetry is found in her prose, notably *Pilgrim at Tinker Creek*. (And indeed she acknowledges her debt to Thoreau in keeping a "meteorological" journal of the mind.) Much of *Pilgrim* is prose poetry, expressing thoughts that fly beyond our immediate grasp but settle slowly into our psyche, evoking in turn a unique emotional connection to some part of nature. Through her observational process, Dillard achieves the immediacy of self to object in a creative and dynamic correspondence to the *exakte sinnliche Phantasie* that Goethe urged as a basis for scientific observation. Scott Slovik sees *Pilgrim* as a form of psychological expression fitting well with some parts of William James's *Varieties of Religious Experience*, and indeed, Dillard's writing contains all of the Jamesian criteria for mystical experience.[248]

TED HUGHES, PRIMEVAL BARD

I read Ted Hughes and feel the raw guts of nature that stir deep inside me ancient memories of the primeval past.

The late Poet Laureate of Britain grew up, as did Wordsworth, in rural England, but in a wilder area, West Yorkshire. Hughes, strongly influenced by the local traditions of bards and Druids, wrote often about Brigit, Celtic nature deity and goddess of poetry. Two centuries after Wordsworth, he created nature poetry of even more mystical expression. Many consider him to be among the greatest of contemporary poets and the first among modern nature poets.

The poems in *River* (1983) reveal this mystical connection to ancient Celtic lore, to creatures of myth and legend, to fish and fishing, and to the savagery of animal life, including human instincts. Hughes expresses a shamanic reverence for the Salmon of Wisdom and other creatures of Celtic myth.[249] A passionate angler, he also addresses the savage part of our nature, as when he faced the accusations of ecopoets as a betrayer of his social obligations toward nature conservation ("You bastard!" exclaimed one poet, outraged over his description of the death throes of a captured salmon).[250]

The maternal reflection of the river, also heard in Wordsworth's lines, resonates in "September": "In this river / Whose grandmotherly, earth-guarded, sweetened hands / Welcome me with tremblings, give me the old feel / Of realities reassurance." And, from the title poem in the collection, "Fallen from heaven, lies across / The lap of his mother, broken by world."

In "Go Fishing," Hughes's abrupt, unromantic verse contrasts with Wordsworth's pastoral poetry but nevertheless convey a deep connection to earth and water:

> Join water, wade in underbeing
> Let brain mist into moist earth
> Ghost loosen away downstream
> Gulp river and gravity.
> Lose words
> Cease
> Be assumed into the womb of lymph
> As if creation were a wound
> As if this flow were all plasm healing.[251]

He joins his quarry, the salmon, wading into the river as spent spawners gulp from hypoxia (caused by the necrosing gills) and die, ghosting downstream, rejoining the womb of water and earth that renews the life cycle.

Hughes's explanatory notes to his poetry reveal his meticulous absorption in the subject matter of the poem. For example, his notes for the poem "Rain-Charm for the Duchy" record the topography and hydrography of the salmon rivers in Devon as only a keen and passionate observer and participant can, vividly describing the spawning habits of the salmon that ascend these rivers. And, as is so characteristic of his mystic naturalism, he writes,

> One of the rewards of…an obsessive salmon fisher is that salmon remain installed in some depth of your awareness, like a great network of private meteorological stations, one in every pool you know, in every river you ever fished, in that primitive underworld, inside this one, where memory carries on "as if real." You can receive a report from any of these stations at any moment, usually unexpectedly. The motion of a cloud noticed through a window, the sudden stirring of a flower in a mid-city border, can be enough.[252]

That awareness in the depths of the "primitive underworld" of memory emerges into consciousness, "unexpectedly," as do similar mystical encounters in nature. The poet appears sublimely in touch with his environment.

His homage to the lowly eel also shows the deep nature mystic in Hughes:

> Her life is a cell
> Sealed from event, her patience
> Global and furthered with love
> By the bending stars as if she
> Was earth's sole initiate. Alone
> In her millions, the moon's pilgrim,
> The nun of water.[253]

The spawning migrations of eels, traveling thousands of miles, are guided by the stars. The pilgrimage ends when the moon's signals dictate the primeval union in the remote sea. Hughes's knowledge of biology enhances his mystic appreciation of nature's rites of passage.

The circle of life and death expresses Hughes's exuberant vitalism that can burn into the reader's feelings. From the orgiastic turmoil of living that fascinates him comes, ultimately, the celebration of the life process in an ethereal plane—so different from Wordsworth, yet strangely akin.

PALEOLITHIC LEGACY

We now turn to some of the earliest known art to demonstrate humanity's drive to achieve a higher consciousness. The graceful paint strokes on the bare stone of deep and dark caves tell us that our ancestors had already then transcended their daily needs with new visions.

In the caves of Spain and France we come face to face with the handprints and painting strokes of those forbears from the Upper Paleolithic era. Homo sapiens, by that time, forty-five thousand years ago, appeared very much like what we are today in brain size and stature. The Hunter was in his prime, and his cave art offers a window into that time.

To behold the abode of that remarkable and beautiful work evokes the mystery and presence of our human heritage. Anyone who has entered deep caves experiences an aura of mystery, perhaps fear. Our Paleolithic ancestors explored far into these caves. Most of the art that has been found is located in remarkably remote areas, as distant as a kilometer or more from the ancient entrance.

In *Entering the Stone,* a sensitive observer, the neophyte caver Barbara Hurd, describes the psychedelic experiences of a first-time spelunker. The near-hallucinatory "mind expanding" imagery she experienced in the uncanny dimension of total darkness and silence in deep caves may correspond with what our Paleolithic ancestors experienced.[254] Many who enter deep caves remark on the absolute sensory deprivation. With extended time in such surroundings some may have experiences that verge upon the hallucinatory. Extraordinary sensitivity to any stimulus may occur. It can be imagined how the Paleolithic people responded to this environment and how creative flow may have been enhanced.

Entering such a cave system once, in the Spanish Cordillera, we were guided through vast caverns, now beautifully illuminated, to ever-narrower passages, and finally, a long distance from the entrance, to the wall paintings. The outline of a human hand, traced by ochreous pigment, struck the visitors with awe. No natural light or sound reaches these remote spaces. Imagine the ancient people hesitatingly exploring this mysterium tremendum, threatened by cave bears, yet finally, with the feeble light of tallow lamps, beginning to inscribe symbols and representational drawings, etchings, and paintings on the rock walls and ceilings. The writer Graham Dunstan Martin points out that "by descending into the cave, primitive man reached the void of his own consciousness—the 'ground' of the world—which is found in silence and darkness."[255] That "ground" is the plenum of space conceived by the physicist David Bohm, the ground for the existence of everything.[256] What was the motivation leading to this creativity? The trance of the hunter in stalking his quarry may have led to its expression in those incredibly distant subterranean spaces. Others have claimed that the Paleolithic hunter created these works from a source of spiritual energy, an expression of mystic connection, not just with fellow life but also with the physical world and the heavens of his nightly wonder.[257]

Shamanism may have its origins in the Paleolithic and possibly earlier eras. The act of representation—of pictures, symbols, and eventually language, which are continuous steps in the evolution of humanity—very likely originates from the expression of hidden regions of consciousness in seeking a union with the unknown. This process led also to the theocratic structures that today, for better or worse, form part of the fabric of human society.

This layering of consciousness probably evolved continuously through the tens of thousands of years of humanity's more documented history. The roots of this consciousness, however, may go back to the earliest organized life, Sinnot's source of consciousness (see chapter 2). If conscious thinking can be traced through the animal world to the level of insects, as the animal psychologist Donald Griffin maintains,[258] and to the plant world, as supported by Tompkins and Bird, then a continuous pathway of the evolution of consciousness from the earliest life appears plausible. From what we see today in those caves where Paleolithic peoples ventured, we may speculate, with Graham Dunstan Martin, that "the mystical was with us from the beginning."[259]

HOMAGE TO THE ROCK

From the mysterious art of Paleolithic peoples we come to a contrasting form of human creativity. Natural formations in the landscape such as rocks have probably been venerated and worshiped from earliest times. These rocks can be seen today in the form of megaliths (giant stones) scattered around the world, sometimes rearranged, as at Stonehenge; other times as single, often spectacular objects. This practice appears to date back at least to the beginnings of the agricultural era ten thousand years ago. We can appreciate the enormous efforts that were made to move and place them. In some cases the location and arrangement of rocks were designed with relationship to predicted celestial events such as the winter solstice.

The simplest and most enigmatic of these structures are called *menhir*—large, solitary rocks, sometimes rising vertically to several dozens of feet.[260] Others, such as *dolmen*, have been arranged in formations that surely presage churches and temples.

Upon seeing Stonehenge, I feel perhaps a bit of the awe that the Celtic population experienced, coming from great distances to gaze upon that architectural wonder. The looming majesty of the silent megaliths stirs up numinous feelings, much like the dark echoing silence through the depths of a Paleolithic cave site. Nature is often a mysterious place for us to inhabit. And we, who evolved as tool-using creatures and have acquired talents and compulsions to assemble, build, and erect, once dug out these megaliths and mounted them as objects of veneration. Of course, later came the pyramids of Egypt and Mexico, the giant stone heads of Easter Island, the cathedrals and temples of Europe and Asia, and much more. Perhaps dating from the era of megaliths, we seem compelled to erect substitutes for nature.

In China, the veneration of natural rocks has been woven into its history up to the present and is part of Taoism, Confucianism, and Buddhism. What are the roots of this art form?

The feeling for a harmony with nature has always been vital to the *Tao,* the road leading to spiritual integration and creative fulfill-ment. Taoism considers that there is a spirit in all things, living and non-living. Indeed, a spirit pervades the cosmos. I can readily under-stand this philosophy as I, too, see a rock in a different light. Viewing such a simple and inanimate object can reveal far more than imme-diately strikes the eye. The rock has a history. It has been created out of ancient forces with powers beyond immediate comprehension. Closer to us than the basalts, granites and schists are the "organic" limestones and marbles laid down by my ancestral cells. Aside from its composition, the rock's history is further shown by the furrows, fissures, crenulations, holes and spurs created by the weathering from perhaps thousands or millions of years of wind, rain, frost, and sun.

In his "Auguries of Innocence," William Blake instructs us how "to see the world in a grain of sand." Likewise, a rock has a correspon-dence, as Emerson suggested, in which "Each particle is a micro-cosm, and faithfully renders the likeness of the world."[261] The rock may reveal what existed before the creation of the universe and every event thereafter to the present moment of its contemplation. It is, to the receptive observer, a spiritual being emanating the power, *qi,* that joins the subject to the object, resulting in a cosmic union. This object of nature is not a deity, a thing to be worshiped. The intensity of feeling for its symbolism is rather veneration, a deeply cultural characteristic in the traditional ways of China and Japan. The art scholar George Rowley wrote, "We must never forget that a culture which is sustained on faith in a personal God cannot seek reality in nature, and that the Chinese, without that faith, could find reality in nature beyond our understanding."[262]

Thus an admiration of natural forms, living and static, is a predominant form of Chinese art. The human figure appears to be secondary in much of this art, in sharp contrast to Greek art of the same era.

There are unusual and striking rocks that came to be called scholars' rocks in China because they were most prized by the literati and intellectuals.[263] These are often dramatic rock formations, placed in gardens or parks or mounted on beautifully carved stands and set in places of honor in a scholar's study. Scholars, often in crowded cities, tried to bring in a feeling of nature in the form of gardens and natural rock formations. As seen also in the bonsai of Japanese homes, these arts reached great heights. For the Chinese, the simplicity of a rock could uncannily stimulate the imagination to perceive a microcosmos of the natural world. Rocks can represent to such petrophiles a condensation of nature's potent power that concentrates the natural forces implied in the *Tao.*

Given the right conditions, the observer of the rock enters that dimension of creative energy, a form of meditation that can be transforming. The process can be like Goethe's *exakte sinnliche Phantasie,* connecting the observer through the visualized rock to all nature and beyond. This step in the Way, *Tao,* is that of *Te,* which can bring the participant closer to self-realization. The *Tao* of an individual incorporates the inner and outer worlds, a nature mysticism that appears close to Swedenborg's correspondences.

In this mystical light we can see how "scholars' rocks" are imbued with energy and power (*qi*). A traditional story is told about the great calligrapher and connoisseur Mi Fu (1051–1107). Upon receiving a government appointment at a provincial capital, he shocked the local officials when presenting himself and his credentials, by bowing instead before a nearby famous and revered rock.[264] This event has become part of legend and the scene depicted in paintings and sculptures to this day (see opposite).

The late American sculptor Richard Rosenblum gathered what is considered to be the finest collection of these rocks in the West. He explains the essence of this art in one cogent paragraph:

> Our twentieth-century notions of art tell us that the act of seeing is a form of making. The conceptual process of creating the many and varied forms of Chinese nature art begins with the initial action of seeing or identifying a particularly evocative natural object; but then the process goes one step further, by extracting the object from its original environment. The intention, however, is never to denature that object or to alienate it as a part of nature that is at once complete in itself and representative of a greater whole in both a formal and an organic sense. A scholars' rock, for example, is a little piece of a wrinkle from which you can imagine the whole wrinkle; it's a little piece of rock from which you can imagine the whole rock; it's a little piece of a mountain from which you can imagine the whole mountain.[265]

The scholars' rocks, like the Bonsai, Suiseki, and the Zen stone garden, are, consequently, mere substitutes for and representations of wild nature, our true and ultimate nourishing source. They serve well however to uplift our spirit and renew our mystical connection to nature. Sitting in a room, in a city, blocked from our natural environment, we can experience transcendence, as if on a magic carpet, to the wild.

Mi Fu bowing to the rock. This classical Chinese scene is known and loved to this day. Hanging scroll by Yu Ming (1884–1935). From the Robert H. Ellsworth Collection in the Metropolitan Museum of Art, New York (by permission of the Metropolitan Museum of Art).

Western artists also seek to recreate nature's patterns. The innate pleasure of viewing Nature is seen in the work of the nature-sculptor Andy Goldsworthy. His unique creativity is demonstrated in totally unexpected yet familiar constructions of natural objects that belong to their surroundings. Viewing a simple pile of rocks being submerged by the flood tide, a woven pattern of leaves or branches swaying in the breeze, or a structure of melting snow or ice gives me a deep, comforting pleasure.

Works by artists such as Paul Klee demonstrate the vivid connection with nature, leading through imaginative processes to the unleashing of great creative energy. Betty and Theodore Roszak declare, "The creative imagination returns us to an aesthetic both old and new, to a mode of knowing the natural world which can be the ally of science. The human [being] again becomes an integral part of nature; life and mind become part of a vital matrix as vast and as old as the universe."[266]

Remarkably, even the abstract drip-paintings of Jackson Pollock reflect nature's patterns. An analysis of Pollock's paintings reveals, according to the physicist turned artist Richard Taylor, typical fractal patterns[267]—and fractals, the fragmented, irregular patterns in nature that are predicted by the new scientific field of chaos theory, are being rediscovered in natural settings. They can be seen in the silhouette of a leafless tree, an image that the English mystic Richard Jeffries loved, or patterns of moss, or seaweed on the beach, or clouds and sand dunes. Emerson, strongly moved by Goethe's thinking on the evolution and continuity of form, wrote, "All is in each.... A leaf is a compend of Nature, and Nature a colossal leaf."[268] These patterns are visually pleasing and can generate an evocative emotion similar to that experienced when viewing "great" art. We are thus surrounded by natural patterns that our sensory engrams have perceived for billions of years, since our ancestors first developed the powers to see, smell, hear and feel. The deep pleasure and harmonic vibration of *qi* comes from piercing the veil of artificial form and seeing the essential reality of things.

CREATIVITY

Artistic creativity as a daily activity among an entire cultural milieu is nowadays unusual. My wife, the Jungian psychoanalyst Manisha Roy, and I once spent some time in Bali, near the village of Mas, the center for traditional woodcarving. Nearby we observed the carvers gather every workday morning under an open pavilion. After prayers of dedication to their particular deity in the Hindu pantheon, they proceeded with their work. The men worked silently and with a serious demeanor. It was as if they had fallen into a trance. They seemed to be in another dimension as they slowly shaped beautiful figures with sureness and skill.

Bali is nearly unique in manifesting the creativity of its inhabitants, blessed as they are by natural beauty and abundant crops. Dance and music performances, and the artisan crafts, reflect the deep spiritual dedication to art. The onlooker clearly senses the meditative and ecstatic feelings of the performers and artisans. The poise and calm demeanor of the people in the cultural heart of Bali, their connection to nature and to religious and cultural tradition, indicates that mysticism is a part of their daily life.

This creative union of humanity with nature through occupation survives in a few other cultures around the world. Although often related to religious traditions, ultimately the mystical process of creativity is a personal and individual feeling. It can exalt the dignity of artisanship, and, indeed, of any activity that can transcend the mundane, grinding, and frantic pace that besets so much of the world in its struggle to break through poverty.

There is probably a hidden treasure lode of memories, concepts, and associations in everyone that can provide the material for the creation of a work of art, the solution of a problem, or a better way of washing dishes. This may be why highly creative people often state that "someone else" is guiding their creativity. The musician plays in a sort of trance, the tennis player is "in the zone," the artist's hands are guided by some outer (yet inner) force. In such instances the experience can reach levels of intensity that could be called "mystical."

Although my fellow hunters and anglers seem culturally bound not to display their "soft" emotional feelings (it isn't macho!) I sometimes see their eyes glisten as they talk of their "camps" in Maine, of moments they do not, dare not, describe but that I sense in their terse, oblique references to experiences that may be called ecstatic. In sharp contrast, artists and musicians may openly express the joy of ecstasy without shame. I recall the transports of the late genius Glenn Gould. Nothing seemed to inhibit him from physical expression, the body language of the profound inner feelings stirred up from creating and hearing beautiful music, often, unfortunately, to the distraction of hearers who were not in the same ecstatic plane as the performer. Or I think of how, as I listen to Beethoven's Quartet in C-sharp minor, Opus 131, the andante cantabile movement transmits directly into my soul the sublime feeling of Beethoven's meditative reverie. Perhaps the ecstatic enjoyment of music, deeply imbedded from eons of the hearing of natural sounds, of birds, waterfalls, thunder, and wind, is part of our natural heritage, for even a single note of musical vibration can lead to an ecstatic experience. Music surely evokes incredibly deep feelings, ranging from the primitive ecstatic emotions generated by jungle drums or rap and rock music to sublime harmonies that seem to lift us to a celestial dimension. Great works of music bring us closer to that transcendental plane.

But I have also seen the ecstasy of creative discovery on the face of scientists, as in a 1998 television interview[269] with the British mathematician Andrew Wiles, who had for many years worked on the problem of the proof for Pierre Fermat's Last Theorem. As Wiles recounted his efforts, the radiance of his words and expression convinced me that he had achieved a moment of ecstasy in the sudden finding of the apparent solution. He described it as "an incredible revelation," "indescribably beautiful," "so simple and elegant." His face shone with the joy of the creative solution he had developed.[270] The exhilaration of discovery, whatever its nature, may be one of the keenest emotions that can be experienced, even exceeding that following sexual orgasm or epicurean ecstasy.

The physicist and writer Alan Lightman tells how, after a great struggle in solving a physics problem, he suddenly and spontaneously reached an ecstatic moment of creativity in finding its solution. "Something strange was happening to my mind...I felt weightless...I had absolutely no sense of myself...I was simply spirit, in a state of pure exhilaration." He compared his state of mind to a loss of frictional drag when sailing a boat. At a certain point, when the hull lifts out of the water, the boat is "planing" as the drag approaches near zero.[271]

Walking in the foothills of Portofino, Friederich Nietzsche experienced a rapture (*Rausch*) of inspiration, which he described in detail. It was one of the creative moments that led to *Thus Spoke Zarathustra*. "One hears, one does not seek; one accepts, one does not ask who gives; like lightning, a thought flashes up, with necessity, without hesitation regarding its form—I never had any choice."[272]

The term *passivity* evoked by James and others in mystical experience is part of the creative experience, as James Leuba, the American psychologist and contemporary of William James, explains: "There are few beliefs more widely entertained than that of the passivity of the artist at the supreme creative moment." It as a common dictum that he must wait for "inspiration." That word, so ready upon the tongue in connection with artistic creation, points to the spontaneity, the unexpectedness, of this kind of mental production. Leuba pointed out, "Here the great joy, rising almost to ecstasy, follows the illumination as a rational consequence of its perceived significance. It is the ecstasy of Archimedes, running naked through the streets of Syracuse after having discovered the principle of specific gravity, shouting 'eureka, eureka!'"[273]

Creativity and mystical experience are transcendent states of mind that lie in the same dimension of our consciousness, the hidden well of our being, which Goethe recognized when he wrote, "All productivity of the highest kind, every important conception, every discovery, every great thought which bears fruit, is in no one's control, and is beyond earthly power. Such things are to be regarded as unexpected gifts from above, as pure divine products."[274] Thoreau described in moving detail the origins of his ecstatic feelings in nature, "an indescribable, infinite, all-absorbing, divine, heavenly pleasure"—yet he knew that he had nothing to do with them, that they were given to him "by a superior Power."[275] The achievement of mystical ecstasy, in nature or anywhere, is a form of cognition beyond the mundane. And the psychologist Andrew Greeley wrote of it as a form of spiritual security, quoting from an epiphany of the writer John Buchan: "It was like a glimpse of the peace of eternity."[276]

9. The Future Rests with Us

For the most part, our society remains embedded in the Western worldview, which isolates us from the natural community and leaves us spiritually alienated from nonhuman life. We have created for ourselves a profound and imperiling loneliness.

RICHARD NELSON, *Searching for the Lost Arrow*

To her fair works did Nature link
The human soul that through me ran;
And much it grieved my heart to think
What man has made of man.

WORDSWORTH, "Lines Written in Early Spring"

ECOCRISIS

WE, AS HUMAN beings, take up so little space in this world—calculations show that our present world population of 6.6 billion individuals could be stacked, like cordwood, out of sight in a corner of the Grand Canyon![277] Yet what we do to our environment, through all our tools, devices, chemicals, factories, and other paraphernalia, has already altered the world climate and littered or altered the global surface. Small though we are, our footprint covers the Earth.

The burgeoning world population and vast movements from rural to urban settings are leading to a global growth of industrialization that is nearly exponential. As energy consumption of fossil fuels increases, so does pollution. Recently a three-kilometer-thick blanket of smog, consisting of aerosols, ash, soot and other particles that originate from burning forests, crop wastes and fossil fuels was detected overlying the Indian Ocean. The darkly ominous smog appears to have originated from heavily populated areas of the Indian subcontinent, among the most polluted in the world. Such a cloud, according to the U.N. Environment Program, can travel halfway around the world in a week. The likely consequences of such a gigantic smog layer include decreased surface temperatures, geographically varied extremes of rainfall and drought, and respiratory illness of all breathing creatures. Nobel laureate Paul Crutzen estimates that up to two million people in India alone are dying prematurely per year from atmospheric pollution.[278] He also believes that such a "blanket" of smog actually retards global warming through the "parasol" effect. Thus it represents a "coiled spring" that may pop out like a jack-in-the-box if the "parasol" of smog is reduced by environmental measures. The acceleration of global warming can then be rapid and amount to an increased mean global temperature rise of as much as two degrees centigrade.

The greenhouse effect and the reduction of the ozone layer are also combining to lead to a drastic alteration of our environment. Rising ocean levels will drown out low-lying islands of several Pacific and Indian Ocean cultures within this century. Montana's Glacier National Park will soon be glacierless, all 150 glaciers totally gone within thirty years. The Aral Sea in Central Asia, once the world's fourth largest inland body of water, will totally disappear, all sixty thousand square kilometers, according to current predictions, by 2015. The gradual disappearance has been caused by decades of misguided irrigation and other agricultural schemes. One ecologist labels this as an "unprecedented anthropogenic impact on nature." Similar changes are occurring in the magnificent Lake Chad. Are our Great Lakes far behind?

What remains for the hunter in this world? The domestication of animals and the subsequent depletion of territory for wild game are squeezing out the few remaining opportunities to relive and renew our connections with wilderness. Fish, likewise, are disappearing from oceans, rivers, and lakes, depleted usually by our insatiable appetite, by pollution, and by the introduction and proliferation of unwanted exotic species.

Who could have imagined that once pristine urban areas such as the San Francisco Bay Region with generally prevailing westerly winds could be overcome at times by smog blankets? The large cities of Asia and South America are seen now from the air covered by immense brown layers extending many miles beyond their borders. Many rivers of Russia and China flow yellow and green with chemical wastes. Lakes and glaciers are disappearing all over the world. The immense solid green expanse of the Amazonian Basin is seen from the air is shorn by great swathes of yellow deforestation. The foothills of Northern India and Nepal are, like shorn sheep, denuded of trees. I have seen these changes.

They are happening everywhere to the glorious and verdant forests that have bedecked our global terra firma, at their maximum dimensions about eight thousand years ago, the beginning of humanity's agricultural era. Now less than half of the world's forests remain, with destruction particularly severe in the last fifty years. E. O. Wilson estimates that the number of species decreases by the fourth root of forest area; which means that when the habitat declines to one-tenth of the original area there follows an extinction of one-half of the species of fauna and flora.[279]

Will it all end as it did on Easter Island (Rapa Nui)? That once thriving creative civilization destroyed itself by cutting down every tree, thus terminating its obsessive program of building and transporting the moai, the great statues that now stand or lie scattered in silent condemnation of an unthinking society. Without our advantage of hindsight, the human society of Rapa Nui gradually and obliviously committed cultural suicide. There is an increasing interest in the history and fate of the Easter Islanders, for the simple reason that what happened to them could happen to us!

Human society is sliding down a slippery slope of environmental destruction toward an ominous future. The political assault on carefully erected safeguards of our environment by some governments is, in Bill McKibben's words, "so large as to be numbing." The rate of the present process of environmental degradation is so slow in terms of human life spans, however, that most of us are not aware of it. In my own lifetime, now coming to a close, I have seen the changes over more than a half century in several increasingly troubled urban and rural parts of the world.

The wasteful expenditure of energy among many countries is vividly apparent, the United States and Europe leading by far. In an impressive but disturbing photographic montage of the Earth as it appears at night, the online image catalog *Visible Earth* (visibleearth.nasa.gov) shows the pattern of electrical lighting seen from space. Because of the reflection of this lighting on our atmosphere, NASA estimates that over one-half of the population of the northern hemisphere cannot see the Milky Way, the galactic nebula to which we belong. This is only a small part, but a poignant symbol, of humankind's blind journey of alienation from nature. Our former Vice-President Al Gore has captured and dramatized much of this looming global catastrophe on film and in print in his acclaimed film, *An Inconvenient Truth.*[280]

Not only our humanoid ancestors but also that primordial blob of protoplasm emerging from the young Earth's hot soup sensed that same bright heaven. As consciousness developed, so surely came the feeling of a cosmic connection. Now, in a cosmic iota of time, our so-called advanced civilization is burrowing ever deeper into warrens of urban expansion. We emerge blindly, like moles, and, bumping into each other, pursue the meaningless tasks of constructing more hovels and acquiring all the chattel that is associated with an "expanding" society. Abandoning the ancient bonds to our natural life, our species is creating a totally different existence based upon the technology that science has brought and that depends entirely upon the exploitation of our natural resources. We are more profoundly perplexed about ourselves than were our ancestors, according to the biologist Edmund Sinnot, who states in his credo, "Postmodern man...is on the verge of spiritual and moral insanity. He does not know who he is."[281]

The Finnish philosopher Georg Henrik von Wright would say that we are escaping into a state of *hubris* that threatens to exceed the limits, the measure (*metron*), of our capacity to live a balanced life and will thus invoke the power of the Greek deity Nemesis. Back in the 1980s, Wright stimulated strong controversy in Scandinavia when he expressed his "provocative pessimism" about humanity's future upon planet Earth.[282]

Wright foresaw an ultimate and probably irreversible clash between industrialization and world ecology. In his thoughtful analysis *Science and Reason,* he asked, is our awareness of the ecocrisis enough reason to expect the present dominating trends to stop or change? His answer was no. Global industrialization, Wright predicted, will continue, and everyday life will only become more dependent on advanced technology, on mechanized production and roboticized services. In short, the scientific-based industrial technology continues its "giddy dance of bacchanalian frenzy" toward the future. Wright foresaw that the environment will be further polluted and ravaged, and artificial products and new forms of energy will replace its disappearing resources. The "explosive rate" of urbanization will be accompanied, as the biologist David Suzuki agrees, by "a deterioration of the social fabric that held people together." Consumerism and materialism rather than social goals will drive government and corporate policies that make us "strangers in the world."[283]

As humanity becomes ever more subject to nature's "revenge," Wright has said that conscientious economists and enlightened statesmen will continue to discuss "a new world economy," the need for "constructive North–South dialogue," "respect for human rights," and other attractive ideals and utopias. But he found it difficult to believe that these will have more than a marginal influence in the immediate future as safety valves for humanity's guilty feelings, or as a dreamscape generated by inadequately fulfilled wishes.

Wright foresaw one possibility, not unrealistic, "that humanity disappears as a zoological entity." That possibility has often been considered in historical times of unrest and change. But he thought the threat had become greater than ever before, though he did not find it especially disturbing. Someday, without any doubt, "Homo sapiens as a species will no longer exist." From a cosmic perspective, Wright said, the significance of whether this happens after a few hundred thousand years or after mere centuries is not worth "a pinch of snuff." When one considers the number of species of life that humankind has eliminated, then such revenge by nature could perhaps be considered just.

But the extinction of humanity is not the only option. Another is that humankind will adopt lifestyles that many will see as "unnatural" or "inhuman." For example, to colonize space, or eliminate, i.e., "rationalize away," classes of the population that technological development has found superfluous in an industrial society. We are already seeing this in the famines, wars, and epidemics that are striking parts of the world not engaged in the industrial globalization. These often result from neglect, willful or otherwise, by industrial powers.

REASON AND LOVE

As for the possibility that there is an instinct strong enough to raise a collective protest to stop the present trend and to lead developments in another direction, Wright considered the protests and the activism of the ecologically concerned green movements, and sympathized with many of them. They represent our civilization's "bad conscience" reminding us that our values are at risk of being lost. But he deplored what he called their tendency toward irrational and chaotic behavior, and said they have not articulated their case well enough to hold the future in their hands.

He is not the only one to make this complaint. One outspoken critic of the "back to nature movement," the American Marxist philosopher Murray Bookchin, accuses the "mystical ecologists" of advocating a return to primitivism and the ways of Paleolithic humans. Certainly there are those who seek and sometimes live the primitive life, who practice ancient rites in the effort to merge with the spirit of Gaia. Bookchin writes of "the proliferation of wiccan covens, Goddess-worshipping congregations, assorted pantheistic and animistic cults, 'wilderness' devotees and ecofeminist acolytes."[284]

As we increasingly realize, the era of the ancient hunting societies was marked by the devastating attenuation and disappearance of wild game populations. Bookchin calls these ancient hunters "predatory opportunists...no less than wolves or coyotes." Humanity, aggressive and thoughtless, exploited our natural resources from the very beginning of its existence. There is ample evidence now of the elimination of large numbers of animal species during the reign of the Paleolithic hunter, the loss of forests in the agricultural era, and the depletion of everything in modern times. So much, says Bookchin, for the romantic image of ancient (as well as modern) humanity, "the mystical path of oneness with nature" and the "timeless, ahistorical misty island of the Lotus Eaters."[285]

It is simplistic perhaps to call for a "return to nature." But I believe that the majority of nature lovers who have experienced a certain spiritual connection—some of whom are quoted in this book—are more grounded in everyday reality. They have developed, in contrast apparently to materialistic thinkers such as Bookchin, an emotional connection with nature that can catalyze the rational actions needed to preserve our environment.

Wright's hope, "if I have one," was toward a protest developing from the "rational component of humanity." He noted the recent re-evaluation of scientific approach that has been taking place in physics and biology—yet, unable to predict how these trends will develop or what role that they will play in history, he hesitated to place much faith in this small sole hope, this "triumph of reason."

Indeed, in this battle reason must face what Michael Polanyi has called "an absurd vision of the universe."[286] Apocalyptic visions of the future that humanity faces are not, of course, new. Ancient religions are rife with predictions of fiery destruction of the Earth and all that live on it. Anthony Stevens describes how the notion of apocalypse can be attractive to those who are deeply troubled by the present state of existence. Global catastrophe pervades the myths and sagas of numerous cultures. The Nordic Ragnarök, like the blink of Brahma's eye, predicts the cyclic end of humanity in fiery chaos, from which a new beginning arises, over and over again. As Stevens asserts, "The cataclysm is inflicted by the gods as punishment for man's transgressions."

From a cosmological and scientific understanding these ancient predictions may be true—millions of years hence. But, disturbingly, among sects of at least two great religions, Islam and Christianity, there are evidently millions of believers who await the end of the world within historical time. Such is a fundamentalist Christian doomsday called the Rapture.[287] Those caught in its apocalyptic vision believe that only true followers of Jesus will be saved for eternity. It is apparent to anyone that such individuals, obsessed by religious hatred of "unbelieving" fellow human beings, can hardly be expected to care "a pinch of snuff" for the problems of our deteriorating environment. The shackles that bind religious fundamentalism to superstition and myth can only be released through scientific knowledge to embrace a meaningful world, our own Earth community.

Wright may well hedge his bet of reason being the hope for the future. But what he has neglected or ignored, it seems to me, is the component of emotion, the love that stems from deep spiritual encounters in nature. The Norwegian philosopher and "deep" ecologist Arne Naess introduced the term ecosophy (Greek: *oikos*="house"; sophia="wisdom") to express a comprehensive understanding of the foundation of life on Earth and the emotional and genetic identification of human beings with all life.[288] Naess makes the connection between our love of life on this planet and our responsibility to nurture it.

Humanity clearly understands that all life is part of the world we share. A rational analysis, therefore, of the accelerating trend toward a global ecological crisis should arouse feelings for the preservation of the environment. Those feelings should in turn lead us to actions to avert our own demise. But Stephen Jay Gould was right when he said that ultimately we will only preserve what we love. We may love only what we understand, and that understanding may come ultimately through education and the experience of uncovering the deep, innate love for life, our biophilia. The more time we spend in nature, the more it enters our feelings. It is why the deep ecology of Arne Naess and his global colleagues is a passionate philosophy that serves as an "academic and political expression of nature mysticism."[289]

The love of the natural world that supports us as a species gives rise to a common sense that moves us to support nature in return. Together, this love and this reason are the necessary ingredients for action to avert the looming catastrophe.

10. Where Are We Headed?

"The West of which I speak is but another name for the Wild:
and what I have been preparing to say is, that in Wildness is
the preservation of the World."

THOREAU, "Walking"

"In the deepest mystical sense, nature is hungry for our
prayers.... We are like a window of the house of nature through
which the light and air of the spiritual world penetrates into
the natural world."

SEYYED HOSSEIN NASR, *The Spiritual and Religious
Dimensions of the Environmental Crisis*

FINDING THE ROAD

MUCH HAS BEEN written about meditative practice, breathing
techniques, yoga, tai chi, and many other exercises that can
lead toward enlightenment or individuation or just calmness. But, for
me, nothing takes the place of being in a natural place. It can be the
seashore, a grove next to a stream, a desert, a snow-clad mountain, or
a coral atoll. It is there, anywhere in pristine nature, where my spirit
spontaneously soars, as it can for most of us.

So I go on beating the drum of my theme, joining many others
far more experienced and articulate in matters of environmentalism.
To really feel strongly about our environment, to have a deep emotional connection, we need to revive and disseminate the concept of

humanity's spiritual connection to nature with its mystic roots. The ecstatic perception of nature, though often in solitude, is a rediscovery of the union of the self with all creation.

If we acknowledge, as did Thomas Aquinas, that all our actions are motivated by some benefit to ourselves we can see how love, the emotional identification with an object, will lead naturally to desire to preserve and nurture it. As the Irish anthropologist Kay Milton writes, "Identification makes morality redundant because we care for ourselves, and whatever is part of ourselves, by inclination, without the need for moral exhortation. Anyone who identifies with natural things, who sees them as part of themselves, is therefore likely to feel inclined to protect them."[290]

To address the immediate trends of self-destruction, we cannot wait for the evolution of our collective consciousness toward a possibly more enlightened and rational state. In a practical sense, the main hope is that we muster our present resources of consciousness in order to propagate throughout our small world the awareness of our potential fate. Georg von Wright considers our fate to be "not worth a pinch of snuff." A philosopher can say that. Mortal beings with instincts of self-preservation and racial propagation willy-nilly must seek solutions.

There is a mental space, a mindset, we create when pondering the intense feelings associated with nature and its degradation by humanity.[291] Shierry Weber Nicholsen suggests that curiosity and attentiveness to our mental space can result in creative links to our inner world. This can become a creative mystic process whereby we allow our inner consciousness to meet the challenges imposed by our own actions. We have the potential capacity to channel incredible energy into creative ventures. Yet, often it seems that we feel drained. As David Peat suggests, this is because we divert the available energy into uncreative paths. We have acquired a vast and heavy baggage of rigidity, a reluctance, even fear to change, from paths that have been firmly carved in our psyches for hundreds of generations. The benefits of scientific materialism surround us and blind many to the hazards of the continued uncontrolled "progress" further degrading our natural environment. The course of that "progress" is like the linear momentum of a huge ocean liner, difficult to stop or suddenly change its course.

Stephen Jay Gould wrote, "We cannot win this battle to save species and environments without forging an emotional bond between ourselves and nature—for we will not fight to save what we do not love."[292] Or, as David Abram puts it, the environmental ethic will not come through the "logical elucidation of new philosophic principles and logistic strictures" but "through a rejuvenation of our carnal, sensorial empathy with the living land that sustains us."[293] And the naturalist George Schaller reminds us, "We're not saving the panda because of biodiversity. We're saving it because it arouses our emotions."[294] Although the feeling part of us will ultimately make that necessary, lifesaving step towards preservation of the biosphere, rationality too must enter the equation. Unfortunately, the consciousness of humanity may sleep until it is awakened by some devastating ecological blow, leaving us little room for any motivation other than fear.

The mysticism of nature and solitude, of love of life and humanity, and of self-awareness is a healing and nurturing state of mind that environmentalists could promote in the efforts to connect the public with the natural environment. I truly believe that it is an inherent positive adaptive mechanism, adjusting our often frantic and aggressive behavior to the slow and stately pace of nature's tempo, thus allowing us to maintain a spiritual connection that gives us comfort and peace.

Bringing Home Nature

The subjective world, our inner state, is that of true reality and is tacit. It is immeasurably greater than our span of rational comprehension. It can be compared to the vast sea of the subconscious that James describes, ebbing and flowing upon the shores of waking consciousness. This expansion of thought, often experienced in the magical moments surrounded by the quiet vastness of the wild, can enable us to see beyond the boundaries of our immediate world and to perceive the nature of the cosmos.

At times, this tacit, subjective part of my self seems to surface and engage the sentient world that is all around. I hunger for solitude, seeing, hearing, smelling the trees, plants, the rivers and oceans, mountains and plains and deserts after too long a stay in the sterility of urban surroundings. That hunger is as real as the hunger for food. It seems an innate feeling, yet conditioning in one's development is surely important. Wordsworth and W. H. Hudson, born and raised in rural settings at nearly opposite ends of the world, both created beautiful structures of words to sanctify their kinship with the nature that they experienced and loved in their youth. That conditioning, that exposure, particularly in youth, to the blessings of wildness and fellow life, is withering as urbanization continues its relentless direction.

Yet, paradoxically, urbanization also holds the potential to benefit our overburdened and exploited natural environment. The centripetal forces of migration from countryside to city throughout the world tend to relieve the pressure on land usage. In the history of New England, the deforestation that occurred in the eighteenth century is now largely reversed following the migration of settlers to more fertile lands in the West, and into the cities following industrialization.

If cities can be cleaner, wastes recycled, pollution minimized, then the often ravaged countryside will have the chance to rejuvenate, threatened species recover and nature to return, slowly, to its wild state. Environmentalist Stephen Kellert asserts, "The current lack of meaningful contact with nature in the modern city and suburb reflects a deficiency of imagination rather than an intrinsic flaw of modern urban life."[295] He refers, however, to affluent communities that can afford to improve the contact with nature in their urban milieus. For example, I live now in the middle of a highly urbanized city but can find refreshment and solace by a walk to the river and its flanking parkways. In contrast, I visit a historic city in India that, fifty years ago, was pleasantly laid out with boulevards, parks and gardens, with clean water and atmosphere. Today, with a fivefold increase of population, it is choking on itself. The sidewalks are not walkable, either from decay or obstruction by innumerable shops, vendors and parked vehicles. Walking on the streets is a limb-and-life-threatening hazard. To get from place to place, even short distances, vehicles of one sort or other must be used. It is a vicious cycle, the less the walking access, the more the vehicles, belching soot and gases, making pedestrian life even less possible. Lakes and ponds, once sparkling blue, are poisonous green, stinking, and refuse-laden. From a perspective overlooking the city, the choked roads are continuously filled with an immeasurably long line of vehicles, sharply evoking the image of ants on an anthill. Inhabitants tend to look the other way, pointing proudly to sweeping modern landscaped business and residential complexes in the environs, a result of India's economic boom. Will the inner city be abandoned some day, as American industrial cities were a few decades ago?

Thus the world crisis may not be solved in the short term by the technology that makes our urban life possible. More people mean more demands on energy, food, and water. Great cities have seldom coped adequately with the problems of industrial pollution and water conservation and reusage. More food means more cropland, not less. And think of the struggling chaos of megalopoli in much of the world where economic reality submerges esthetic value and diesel soot coats the sparse greenery. A breaking point in Gaia's tolerance is fast approaching.

PASSING THE TORCH

Wordsworth saw the ultimate source of truth in the innocence of childhood, uncorrupted by the mundane and ever increasing pollution of materialistic positivism. I also plead for the realization that our children, our hope for the future, should increasingly feel, hear, see and touch what constitutes our natural world. That is the only way they can nurture the innate instincts to cherish and love our world with all its diversity.

There is a powerful spirituality in children that is not always recognized. Memories of childhood ecstasies can be profound and everlasting. Near-death experiences and the spiritual revelations of dying children have been documented by Elisabeth Kübler-Ross in remarkable and touching accounts. The psychologist Edward Hoffman made a revealing study of childhood spirituality by interviewing adults about their early experiences—a significant number of which occurred while in the out-of-doors, in wilderness, the countryside, farms, seashore, etc.

Many of these experiences resemble the mystical encounters recorded earlier in this book. For example, the phenomenon of photism was frequent. A teenager walking through the Nova Scotia countryside suddenly felt "tremendously elated, and then euphoric. Simultaneously the entire world seemed to be suffused with a tremendous light."[296] Other experiences included a unitive feeling. At age four a girl was standing on the seashore, watching breaking waves, when suddenly "A door opened, and I became the sun, the wind, and the sea.... Sound, smell, taste, touch, shape—all melted into a brilliant light."[297]

An eleven-year-old Little Leaguer experienced the sense of slowing of time:

> On the next pitch, something happened. As the pitcher began his regular windup, the illumination on the field seemed to become brighter, and everything became silent and luminous. Everything went into slow motion. The pitch came, and the ball floated in as big as a basketball. I hit it squarely...ran to first, tumbled into the grass, and laughed until I cried.[298]

According to Hoffman, many more people than we suspect may have undergone peak or mystical experiences in their early years. The 250 episodes that he analyzed met many of the criteria of mystical experience. It seems, too, that these ecstasies led to or were part of profound changes in the interviewee's life style or worldview.

Childhood is often the time when the passion of spiritual experience seems greatest. Christian de Duve, 1974 Nobel laureate in medicine, remembers:

> On a clear summer night almost seventy-five years ago, I was sitting...with a group of...youngsters circling a fire.... The flames rose straight toward an inky sky studded with stars...All of a sudden, for a brief instant, light fused with darkness, song and silence became one, and I felt carried to another world, seizes by intense emotion, suffused with a sense of unfathomable mystery, feeling, beyond the infinite depths of space, the awesome majesty of God.[299]

In E. L. Doctorow's short story "Willi," the protagonist, recalling his youth, walks in the fields and imagines the Earth's soul enveloping him in a divine embrace: "I fell at once into a trance and yet remained incredibly aware.... Such states come readily to children. I was resonant with the hum of the universe." That episode, demonstrating all the Jamesian criteria for mystical experience, could surely (and perhaps did in Doctorow's case) lead to a lifelong memory and a continuing respect and love of nature.

My own childhood memories are strongly imprinted with experiences in nature: splashing up streams and finding mysterious creatures under rocks, wading in tidal pools and being astonished by brilliantly colored anemones, walking through quiet, cool forests of gigantic redwoods, and hunting oddly shaped fungi. Later a children's microscope brought a whole new world into my senses. Such memories last forever.

But the increasing alienation from nature experienced by children in the urbanizing world society has led, at least in America, to what the social thinker and journalist Richard Louv calls the Nature Deficit Disorder.[300] Childhood experiences of playful romps and explorations through meadow and forest are replaced by competitive games on paved playgrounds and, increasingly in this technological age, television viewing (the figures for children are staggering), computer games, and other electronic pastimes that can lead to "social autism." One fourth-grader told him, "I like to play indoors 'cause that's where all the electrical outlets are." Louv speculates about a relationship of the epidemic of attention deficit hyperactivity disorder (ADHD) with the alienation from nature and presents evidence to show that reconnecting children with nature will dramatically improve their behavioral symptoms.

Childhood nature experiences do relate to future adult environmental attitudes. One study shows clearly that early participation in "wild nature" leads significantly to positive adult environment activism. "When children become truly engaged with the natural world at a young age, the experience is likely to stay with them in a powerful way—shaping their subsequent environmental path," according to the Cornell investigators.[301]

Childhood experiences in nature can also include moments of fear, of being lost or threatened by strange beasts, by terrifying gales or blizzards. The varying aspects of natural experience lead toward spiritual maturation, toward a worldview in which an individual may realize that the values of good and evil are human ideas, that the natural world is neutral with respect to anthropocentric morality. According to Louise Chawla, ecstatic environmental memories from childhood can lead, through the imagination, to the foundation for a firm footing in life and to a mature philosophy of nature.[302]

Those of us lucky enough to have early exposure to life in the outdoors have generally been infected with the spirit of environmental consciousness. Our innate sense of biophilia is in full flower. When we have felt a transcendent experience in nature (and I speak for myself) we are "hooked" for life. That permanent memory becomes a guide to returning the favor to Mother Nature, to respect, preserve, and restore that which has been damaged or lost through the artificial and destructive actions of humankind.

Depending on our station in life these ethics can range from the simple *primum non nocere* (first do no harm) of the physician's credo to sweeping influences upon national and international policies. One responsibility that can have long-lasting benefits is the teaching of natural and environmental history and encouraging the direct participation of youth in wilderness experience. As I have mentioned, many such programs exist in developed countries and many are beginning in other parts of the world. This learning experience at an early stage will have great benefits for future environmental awareness.

The psychologists Rachel and Stephen Kaplan studied the impact of an extended and organized nature program upon young people, many coming from urban settings. The investigators found several changes in the group, particularly the "remarkable depth of spiritual impacts" and the "recovery of aspects of mental function that had become less effective through overuse."[303] Perhaps those solitary moments in the wild created the apophatic conditions of mystical feeling that could lead to renewed creativity.

How can such experiences come to urban youth? They may well represent the key to our future. We have seen examples of the innate spirituality of children and of their joyous immersion into the bountiful arms of Nature. The environmental consciousness of youth, if developed, may be a principal weapon against the direction the entire world is taking toward consumerism and materialism, a force for the preservation and restoration of the biosphere and of our collective psyche.

The urban life may foster the development of a quick and precocious intelligence but at the cost of eliminating the rich range of experience that should be the heritage of all humanity. Our senses are deprived of their natural stimuli. Civilization has trapped many of us into cocoons of our own making, leading us to meaningless internecine conflicts while our own wild selves live underground, dormant and despairing.

ROADBLOCKS

The uncontrolled sprawl of urbanization is forming a blot not only on our global landscape but also upon the collective mind of humanity. Wordsworth, over two hundred years ago, agonized, that "...a multitude of causes, unknown to former times, are now acting with a combined force to blunt the discriminating powers of the mind."[304] These forces included "the increasing accumulation of men in cities" with their craving for "extraordinary incident" that needed hourly gratification and a "degrading thirst after outrageous stimulation."

For decades thoughtful analysts have argued that the head-long consumerist-based path of industrialization must be radically altered. Their arguments have been met with excuses and explanations couched in pretty words of the impossibility of such change. But more and more individuals appear to have become aware of the need for change. The confidence in the present system is waning, and many are liberating themselves from the old mentality of waste and pollution.

The spiritual devastation of the blights of unplanned urbanization, it seems, is the root of much that ails us. There are and have been violent and brutal conflicts in rural areas around the world. Human nature contains a streak of cruelty and brutality that is no less than and may exceed that of most fellow creatures. The zoologist Matt Ridley has hopes, however, that in the case of humanity, "The roots of social order are in our heads, where we possess the instinctive capacities for creating not a perfectly harmonious and virtuous society, but a better one than we have at present."[305] Deep inside us, as with other social beings, is the instinct for self-preservation that can transcend our mundane search for gratification. That instinct may come down to us from billions of years of pragmatism, knowing that cooperation, not competition, will save the community. But all depends upon what each of us considers our community. Family, caste, religion, nation, or the entire human world? This morality is our heritage and potential savior. In which direction is it going? Probably to all points of the compass. Wanton cruelty is counterpoised by magnanimous altruism and gentleness, with all degrees of these qualities around the compass rose. Can we steady the wobbling compass toward a common, global, and humanitarian goal?

NEEDED: THE MORAL EQUIVALENT OF WAR

We are now near a threshold of decision. The loss of natural habitat, the increase of population and industrialization are pushing us toward a kindling point. Suffering from disease and war will not go away despite our technological advances and superior intellects. The connection to our Mother Nature has largely been lost. Whole generations of human beings in this world have scarcely seen a forest, a flowering valley, or a wild animal.

Biophilia is our key to the door of perception behind which we see that nurturing the life and resources of this small planet is our main responsibility. The love affair with nature is like a love affair with the most beautiful woman in the world. The heart claps: the ecstasy is the same, the need to nurture and protect exceeds all else.

Such feelings are nourished by the knowledge of our incredible evolution, along with all other life, to the marvelous complexity and diversity that fills our senses. This knowledge, which has been provided by science, of the vibrant biosphere of this solitary planet provides the ground for the spiritual connection that can lead to a redemption of humanity's heretofore oblivious and exploitative attitude toward the environment.

With almost 6.7 billion human beings on Earth, there are perhaps mere thousands of wilderness activists and only millions of ecologically concerned individuals and members of traditional subsistence cultures. That tiny group of environmentalists must communicate to the immensely larger balance of humanity the messages that can convince all to begin to turn away from the slippery slope of biospheric meltdown.[306] One such message is a women's movement that has come to be called "ecofeminism." In exploring some of the deeper and sexist conflicts in ideas about human evolution, this movement has shown how the nurturing spirit of feminism can counter the destructive, materialistic and masculine side of humankind.[307]Another useful concept is "environmental imagination," the term that the Harvard professor Lawrence Buell uses to describe a process that can "energize" thought and action toward renewed engagement with nature.[308]

Awareness may spring vicariously from reading or hearing of that which is already in front of most of us. Nature writing serves to bring to our attention not just the beauty, structure, and organization of all natural things, large and small, but also the inroads made by humanity in the normally homeostatic and symbiotic biosphere. Visual art, too, can be a powerful heightener of environmental consciousness. The images that Ansel Adams captured in his large-view cameras are eternal reminders of that ecstatic youthful moment on Mount Clark, and those images have in turn captured the hearts and imagination of possibly millions.

Still, only the immediate experience of nature can evoke the sharp jab of consciousness that can penetrate into the inner psyche and move us to act out of an unshakable love for the Earth. As John Muir writes about his beloved Sierra Nevada: "No amount of word-making will ever make a single soul know these mountains."

Major efforts at all levels of society to create programs with direct wilderness experience can imbue youth with the knowledge, respect, and with the spiritual love that Stephen Gould says is the only way to win the battle to save our biosphere. Both "intellectual and visceral journeys" will be necessary to cultivate "biospheric awareness" in the young in order to revive humanity's innate biophilia.[309] In many countries there are flourishing wilderness programs. The Wilderness Awakening School in Washington State is an example. Here the students learn the walking meditation of tracking, the vision quests of the Native Americans, and emerge enlightened and, one hopes, changed forever in feeling their and our unbreakable link to nature. These modern vision quests foster a sense of self-discovery, self-reliance, and regenerate from innate sources a deeply imprinted spiritual connection to nature. Such lasting memories can be refreshed by contact with even small bits of nature; a tree, a garden, even a rock.

In numerous small Nordic communities there are now successful programs for essentially eliminating fossil fuels for power needs, for truly effective recycling, and for nearly total elimination of sources of atmospheric and water pollution. A key to these programs is the commitment by the population to drastically reduce the need for power, a change in lifestyle that can serve as models for the power-hungry giants such as the United States, industrialized Europe, and China.

Can a mystic be a doer as well as a thinker? As I have sought to demonstrate in this book, mystical experience in nature affects a broad spectrum of individuals in a wide range of emotional responses and, ultimately, commitments. Notable examples of American environmental activists and nature mystics are John Muir, Ansel Adams, Aldo Leopold, Bill McKibben, and Henry Thoreau. Yet there are countless unnamed individuals, who do not write books or make speeches, who have felt the magic transformation and who quietly or publicly support and foster environmental conservation. There are no data, but a robust nature mystic can be the next-door neighbor, a member, perhaps, of some environmental or wilderness organization, a hiker, or a hunter.

One personal recollection may illustrate this point. The guide and mountain climber Norman Clyde (1885–1972) was a powerful presence in the Sierra Club. A schoolteacher, he experienced an epiphany early in life when trekking through the Sierra Nevada. He abandoned his profession and chose to live in the mountains for the rest of his life. Although reclusive, prone to solitary mountain ascents at night, achieving numerous first ascents of peaks along the range, he was also an inspiring guide for generations of trekkers and climbers. I recall visiting Norman in his small cabin above Big Pine, incredibly cluttered with gear, yet also containing a select collection of poetry and classic literature. He was not one to express his feelings, yet I sensed a deep spiritual presence akin to that of a *sadhu,* who renounces worldly attachment. But Clyde was no *sadhu.* His activities for the Sierra Club and others showed his active dedication to the preservation of our wilderness. There are untold numbers of people like Clyde, nature mystics who do not renounce the world, but rather engage in it.

We have evolved in a beautiful but sometimes harsh and unforgiving world and have in turn inflicted our violence upon it. We have experienced unending conflict between ourselves. The violence that we inflict on the planet may result in such disequilibrium that the ultimate consequence will be our own demise, at least in terms of the society we know today, a *Götterdämmerung* for humanity.

What additional forces can be mustered for the battle to preserve our biosphere? I turn again to the sagacious William James, who wrote, nearly one hundred years ago but very much to the point of our present crisis: "What we now need to discover in the social realm is the moral equivalent of war: something heroic that will speak to men as universally as war does, and yet will be compatible with their spiritual selves as war has proved itself to be incompatible."[310]

This battle, as Krishna taught Arjuna in the Bhagavad-Gita, was the search for "refuge in the original spirit of man, from which primordial activity extended."[311]

A moral battle is needed, involving the virtues associated with war: selflessness, heroism, and energy. That battle is wholly compatible with our spiritual selves, within which we preserve the deep-rooted feeling for our nourishing wilderness; the life, water, air, and soil from where we emerge and to where we will return.

Georg von Wright's pessimistic statement of humanity's future ends with an epigram from a poem by Goethe:

Noch ist es Tag, da rühre sich der Mann,
Die Nacht tritt ein, wo niemand wirken kann.

(It is still day and humanity can act,
When night comes, nothing can be wrought.)

Goethe was paraphrasing a line from the New Testament, in which Jesus told his disciples, "I must work the works of him that sent me, while it is day: the night cometh, when no man can work" (John 9:4).

It is still day, and there is still time to change course, to renew the emotional bond between nature and ourselves, that fragile bridge in danger of collapse. The potential spiritual majesty of the human soul needs nurturing at the well of nature's beneficence. The psychic qualities that connect us so deeply to nature and to each other are what make us human. Let us act to save them now, for when night comes it will be too late.

Notes

1   Ansel Adams (fragment, no date), quoted by Nancy Newhall in *Ansel Adams,* 16–17.

2   Marghanita Laski described in her groundbreaking book *Ecstasy* the circumstances leading to mystical experience in a survey of sixty-three volunteers. Greeley and McCready, in a larger sample ("Are We a Nation of Mystics?"), corroborated the universality of many characteristics of mystical experience, such as the sensation of unusual light, the alteration of the sense of time ("time stood still") and the feeling of deep and profound peace.

3   Samuel Taylor Coleridge in *Anima Poetae*, Oct. 21, 1803, quoted by Laski in *Ecstasy*, 8.

4   Ibid., 508. At a certain stage of seeking, "the man identifies his real being with the germinal higher part of himself...and becomes conscious that this higher part is coterminous and continuous with a *more* ...which is operative in the universe outside of him..."

5   See Cardena et al., *Varieties of Anomalous Experience*, including the chapter by David M. Wulff on "Mystical Experience," for a discussion of the various states of consciousness from the psychological perspective.

6   Koch, *Quest for Consciousness*, 6.

7   Orr, *For the Love of Life,* 486–7.

8   Alter, *Sacred Waters,* 145. Stephen Alter, born in India, undertook a journey, involving months of trekking, to the sources of the Ganges River high in the Garhwal and Kumaon districts of the new state of Uttaranchal.

9   Devereux, *Sacred Place*, 49. He describes the varieties of natural settings, natural and manmade objects of a sacred and encompassing human geography.

10 Matthiessen, *Snow Leopard,* 115.

11 Nietzsche, *Ecce Homo*, 300.

12 Turgenev, *Hunter's Sketches,* 445.

13   See Cass Adams, *Soul Unearthed,* for descriptions and sources of several current wilderness programs.

14   von Essen, *Revenge of the Fishgod,* 63.

15   See Russel Hvolbek's *Mysticism and Experience* for a further discussion of the impact of nature upon mystical experience.

16   Devereux, *Sacred Place,* 184.

17   Chawla, *Ecstatic Places,* 23.

18   Melville, *Moby Dick,* 4–5.

19   A transcendent passage from Proust's *Swann's Way,* in the Modern Library Edition, 2003, pp. 63–64.

20   Tuan, *Topophilia,* 114–120.

21   Kellert and Wilson. *Biophilia Hypothesis,* 422. Millions of years of human evolution (and billions of years of our entire evolution) have shaped our awareness, our consciousness of nature. "Biophilia is inscribed in the brain itself expressing tens of thousand of years of evolutionary experience." See also Wilson's *Biophilia,* 1.

22   Shepard, *Where We Belong,* xxxii.

23   Goethe, W. v., 1824. In *Schriften zur Wissenschaftslehre.* http//: www.steinerschule-bern.ch/Goethe/wissenschaft/Ernst.htm. Goethe reviews Ernst Stiedenroth's book *Psychologie zur Erklärung der Seelenerscheinungen* and coins the phrase in praising the author, a scientist, for allowing imagination to participate in the process of creative thought, "without which no art is possible."

> So wird ein Mann, zu den sogennanten exakten Wissenschaften geboren und gebildet, auf der Höhe seiner Verstandsvernunft nicht leicht begreifen, daß es auch eine exakte sinnliche Phantasie geben könne, ohne welch doch eigentlich keine Kunst denkbar ist.

24   Bortoft, *Wholeness of Nature,* ix. In the Introduction by Norman Skillen.

25   Emerson, *Nature* (1836), 13. The "transparent eye-ball" metaphor provoked considerable discussion and one famous caricature by his fellow transcendentalist Christopher Pearse Cranch (Figure 2a).

26   J. A. Wheeler, *Bohr, Einstein, and the Strange Lesson of the Quantum* in Elvee, *Mind in Nature.* "I know of no clue more likely to allow us someday to grasp an understanding of these questions [the origin and structure of the universe] than the quantum" (23).

27   Helen Keller had many mystical experiences. She wrote about them, and of her understanding of Swedenborg, in *Light in the Darkness,* edited by Ray Silverman (West Chester, PA: Chrysalis Books, 1994, 15).

28   Buell, *Writing for an Endangered World*, 83. Buell discusses Lopez's
      "dual accountability" (objective representation versus fabulation)
      in his piece on how bears stalk seals (92–93). In a telling aside
      Buell writes, "John Stuart Mill, who found solace in Wordsworth's
      compelling rendition of physical nature, would have been astonished
      by the stinginess of modern argument that Wordsworth reckoned
      nature as at best a convenience and at worst an impediment to the
      imagination" (84).

29   Hodder, *Thoreau's Ecstatic Witness*, quotation from Thoreau's *Journal*.

30   Slovik, *Seeking Awareness*, 49.

31   See Crary's discussion of Goethe, Kant, and Schopenhauer's ideas
      of the role that the senses played in our perceptive and imaginative
      process in his chapter, "Subjective Vision and the Separation of the
      Senses," in *Techniques of the Observer*, particularly 71–81.

32   Thoreau, *Journal*, Dec. 25, 1851, pp. 155–156.

33   Hofmann, *Insight Outlook*, 7.

34   Swedenborg, *Arcana Coelestia*, 4526.

35   PBS, September 29, 1999.

36   Jahner, Elaine. "The Spiritual Landscape." In *Parabola* vol. 2, no.3
      (1977), pp. 32–38.

37   Peirce, *Collected Papers*, 268, cited in Martin, *Shadows in the
      Cave,* 107.

38   Emerson, *Nature* (1836), 36. Ralph Waldo Emerson, ever the teacher
      and somewhat grandiloquent as was Lord Chesterfield, wrote essays
      on many subjects, including a masterpiece on *Nature* from which
      many quotations can be gleaned. However, Emerson's *Nature* has
      been a source of confusion, for me at least, involving many hours of
      tedious bibliographical research. There are, in fact, two distinct essays
      of the same title, written at different times of Emerson's life and of
      vastly different character.

      The first essay, quoted in this chapter, was published in 1836 as a
      book of 94 pages, Emerson's first, entitled *Nature* and consisting of
      eight short chapters. According to several biographers and reviewers,
      it represents the genesis of Emerson's philosophical thesis that later
      became known as Transcendentalism. It is written in lucid prose with
      almost naïve enthusiasm, consistent with Emerson's youth.

      The second essay, widely read in American Lit in high schools and
      colleges, was published in 1844 and was part of a collection of essays
      entitled *Essays, Part Two* of which *Nature* is the sixth and comprises
      27 pages of text. Its prose is more opaque and its character more
      pedantic.

39   Storr, *Solitude*, 28.

40   Ibid., 37.

41 Lindbergh, *Gift from the Sea,* 24, 32, 33.

42 Csikszentmihalyi, *Finding Flow,* 42.

43 Thoreau, *Portable Thoreau,* 602.

44 Ibid., 630. His essay on walking epitomizes the nearly obsessive love of nature that Thoreau experienced in those early days of the American expansion and "taming" of the environment. At that time more than three-fourths of the primeval forest in Massachusetts had been felled. Walden Pond was surrounded by a relatively barren landscape. Today the forest has regained a toehold and over three-fourths of Massachusetts is again wooded. Thoreau might not recognize his haunts along the shores of Walden Pond.

45 It is disconcerting to read from the new ecocriticism and ecogenderism of attempts to sweep away the sincere but often anthropocentric writings of naturalists like Thoreau. For example, Louise Westling in Coupe, *The Green Studies Reader*, chapter 44, discusses "Thoreau's Ambivalence toward Mother Nature":

> Male writers down to our time have reiterated Thoreau's version of American pastoral. Hemingway's Nick Adams and Faulkner's Ike McCaslin perform similar escapist nest-building and killing rituals in eroticized landscapes, and gendered responses to Nature motivate environmentally conscious essayists like Edward Abbey and Barry Lopez. Understanding the destructive gender oppositions in *Walden* should help us see that as long as we continue to feminize nature and imagine ourselves apart from the biota, we will continue to enable the "heroic" destruction of the planet, even as we lament the process and try to erase or deny our complicity in it. (265)

46 Quoted by Richardson, *Emerson,* 155.

47 Swedenborg, *Arcana Coelestia,* 1968 edition (New York: The Swedenborg Foundation, para. 6319).

48 Thoreau, *Journal,* 5:359, quoted by S. Slovik in *Seeking Awareness in American Nature Writing,* 24.

49 E. Taylor, *Shadow Culture,* 63.

50 Thoreau, *Journal,* 3:274–275.

51 Olson, *Singing Wilderness,* 7. Sigurd Olson spent a lifetime exploring the wild lake country of the Quetico-Superior and beyond. His invocation of music as a metaphor for the primeval roots of our search for attachment with nature is echoed in Bruce Chatwin's *Song Lines* of the Australian aborigines.

52 Beston, *Outermost House,* 10.

53   Hudson, *Far Away and Long Ago,* 224–225. Stephen Bodio writes
      in his introduction to Hudson's childhood recollections, "*Far Away
      and Long Ago* is the best of a rare and wonderful genre: the childhood
      autobiographies of literate naturalists" (xiii).

54   Kellert, *Kinship to Mastery,* 41. Stephen Kellert devotes a chapter to
      considering the aesthetics of nature, 33ff.

55   Carl Jung in *Eranos Jahrbuch 1938,* quoted by Laski, 55.

56   Wright, Karen. "Where Did the Moon Come From?" in *Discover,*
      February 2003, p. 65. See also *New Scientist,* August 2004, 27–30.

57   See Michael Boulter's *Extinction,* 61–62. The scientific contributions
      of the Apollo missions were important. The study of moon rocks has
      established the origin of the moon as a fragment of the newly formed
      Earth. Through the calculations of impact and dislodged mass it is
      possible to estimate the forces that may have knocked the Earth off its
      normal axis of rotation.

58   Darwin, *Origin of Species,* 484.

59   Haldane, *On Being the Right Size,* 107. In a chapter entitled *The
      Origin of Life* written before 1932 he stated, "It is probable that all
      organisms now alive are descended from one ancestor." With modern
      techniques of DNA chemistry Haldane's prediction is now surely
      confirmed. Christian de Duve (*Vital Dust*) and Lynn Margulis and
      Dorion Sagan (*Microcosmos*) have written easily understandable
      reviews of these exciting advances in evolutionary biology.

60   Margulis and Sagan, *Microcosmos,* 14. "From the paramecium to the
      human race, all life forms are meticulously organized, sophisticated
      aggregates of evolving microbial life. Far from leaving microorganisms
      behind on an evolutionary 'ladder,' we are both surrounded by them
      and composed of them. Having survived in an unbroken line from
      the beginnings of life, all organisms today are equally evolved."

61   See Andrew Knoll's lucid review of what we presently know (and
      don't know) about the early evolution of life in *Life on a Young Planet,*
      157.

62   See Margulis and Sagan, *Beast with Five Genomes.* They show that
      endosymbiosis did not end just there. Today many organisms have
      been found to have five or more genomes. Life is truly cooperating
      and interpenetrating.

63   Schneider, *Scientists on Gaia,* 13. The present gaseous percentages on
      Mars, that evolved at a similar time with Earth, compared to those
      presently in Earth's atmosphere:

	OXYGEN	NITROGEN	CARBON DIOXIDE
Earth	21	79	0.03
Mars	trace	2.7	95

Climatic conditions resulting from this near-global ocean (in the Achaean period) appear to have been conducive to the origin of life and the "birth of Gaia" at around 3.5 billion years ago (80).

64   Sinnot, *Cell and Psyche,* 61. Edmund Sinnot, Professor of Botany at Yale University, considered the trait of organizing as the distinctive character of all life. He saw slime molds, among the most ancient of organisms, as examples of this ability to organize, i.e. to form colonies and to move. Also, "Biological organization and psychical activity is fundamentally the same thing" (48). His hypothesis was, "The whole conscious life of man—is simply a manifestation of an organized biological system raised to its loftiest levels" (72).

65   Margulis and Sagan, *Microcosmos,* 152. "Again and again, the study of the microcosm brings home to us that human capacities grow directly from other phenomena. Nature has a certain subsuming wisdom; our aptitudes must always remain meager in comparison to the biosphere of which we form relatively tiny parts. But we are not discontinuous from the general path of evolution, from the flows and flux of matter, information and energies. Nor can human thought—the last refuge of those insisting on human 'higherness'—be isolated or dissociated from the prior accomplishments of life."

66   See Bloom, *Global Brain*, which discusses the evolutionary continuity of consciousness.

67   Alfred Binet was a remarkable observer of behavior whose *Psychic Life of Micro-organisms* anticipated his studies of human behavior.

68   Peat, *Synchronicity,* 66–67.

69   Richard Feynmann observed paramecia as a youngster and gave these thoughtful comments in his delightful *Surely You're Joking, Mr. Feynmann: Adventures of a Curious Character* (London: Counterpoint Paperback, 1987, p. 92).

70   Gore, *Earth in the Balance,* 264.

71   "For the first time I saw the horizon as a curved line. It was accentuated by a thin seam of dark blue light—our atmosphere. Obviously this was not the ocean of air I had been told it was so many times in my life. I was terrified by its fragile experience." German Astronaut Ulf Merbold, in *The Home Planet.* Unpaged.

72   Jacob von Uexkuell likened our biosphere to life in a terrarium, nine kilometers high. *Der unsterbliche Geist in der Natur.* Hamburg: Christian Wegner Verlag, 1946. 6.

73   From the article "The Biosphere and Concepts of Ecology" in *New Encyclopedia Britannica Macropedia*, v. 14, 1127–1221 (Chicago: Encyclopedia Britannica). I calculate the biosphere a bit more conservatively than others: add the deepest part of the ocean (11 km)

to the tip of Mount Everest (9 km) and take away 2 (nothing lives on top of Everest).

74   The Earth's equatorial diameter is 12,756 km. Assume that an orange's diameter is 10 cm. If the biosphere were 18 km thick, then its counterpart around the orange would be 0.14 mm.

75   Lovelock, *Ages of Gaia*, 210. "Our bodies contain a veritable history of life on Earth."

76   Teilhard de Chardin, *The Human Phenomenon*, 68. "Taken as a whole, from the first stages of its evolution, the living substance spread over the Earth forming the features of a single, gigantic organism."

77   Emerson, *Nature* (1836), 13.

78   Jeffries, *Story of My Heart*, 19.

79   I am grateful to David Oswald for permission to use his translation of Rainer Maria Rilke's *Sonnets to Orpheus*, Part II, stanza 14.

80   Kellert, *Kinship to Mastery*, 97.

81   Abram, *Spell of the Sensuous*, 131. For Abram, as the animals, plants, and rivers once spoke to our ancestors, the "inert letters of this page" now speak to us. "This is a form of animism...as mysterious as a talking stone."

82   Kahn, *The Human Relationship with Nature*, 7. The author explores evolutionary psychological theory through a series of interviews of various groups of adults and children. He found that young children were limited in their relationship with nature.

83   Shepard, *Traces of an Omnivore*, 68.

84   Shepard, *Where We Belong*, 209.

85   Stevens quotes Desmond Morris, 1969, *The Human Zoo*. London: Jonathan Cape.

86   Thomas, *The Lives of a Cell*, 107ff. Lewis Thomas reported some observations by the anthropologist C. M. Turnbull in *The Mountain People*, New York: Simon and Schuster, 1972.

87   The Zurich psychoanalyst C. A. Meier considered "the unconscious as inexhaustible as nature," that it represented humanity's inner wilderness. From "Wilderness and the Search for the Soul of Modern Man" in the Festschrift *Testament to the Wilderness* (Zurich: Daimon Verlag, 1985, 6).

88   Petersen, *Heartsblood*, 11. "Genetics confirms that as a species we have not had enough time in just 10,000 years of agriculture to evolve one iota of change in our collective genomes."

89   Ortega y Gasset, *Meditations on Hunting*, 150.

90   Ibid., 152. "In fact, the only man who truly thinks is the one who, when faced with a problem, instead of only looking straight ahead, toward what habit, tradition, the commonplace and mental inertia

would make one assume, keeps himself alert, ready to accept the fact that the solution might spring from the least foreseeable spot in the great rotundity of the horizon." See also Maclean's quotation in *A River Runs Through It* (p. 92).

91   Thoreau, *Portable Thoreau, Walden,* 525.

92   Austin, *Zen and the Brain,* 16.

93   Nabhan, *Cultures of Habitat,* 9.

94   Murchie, *Seven Mysteries of Life,* 473. In his encyclopedic overview of our world, Guy Murchie shows how *Homo's* brain has tripled in size in less than one million years, a dramatic change that has exceeded that of all other mammals.

95   Peat, *Synchronicity,* 222. For a perceptive discussion on some roots for the "hunter's trance," read David Peat's section, "The Tiger and the Forest," 221–225.

96   von Essen, *Revenge of the Fishgod,* 22–23.

97   Camuto, *Hunting from Home,* 18. He describes in essence the features of the hunter's trance.

98   See Cartmill, *A View to a Death in the Morning,* for a critical distancing from the theory that hunting is a "natural activity."

99   Stange, *Woman the Hunter,* 187. Her book supports the idea that all humanity, no matter the gender, has inherited similar traits and instincts, and, given the circumstances, will make them manifest. The professional hunter's observations are in an article by Albert Yendes entitled "Contrary to Popular Opinion" in *Petersen's Hunting* (March 1993). 34.

100 Rezendes, *Wild Within,* 71.

101 Corbett, *Jungle Lore,* 21. The legendary hunter describes how his deeply rooted instincts combined with acquired knowledge to deal with the notorious man-eating tigers and leopards he was assigned to kill. He found at least once how the tables were turned when the supposed quarry, the Champawat man-eater, stalked him with nearly fatal results.

102 Rezendes, *Wild Within,* 94.

103 Jonsson, *Inner Navigation,* 321.

104 Hay, *Mind the Gap,* 116.

105 Dillard, *Pilgrim at Tinker Creek,* 184.

106 Nabokov, *Speak, Memory,* 139.

107 Maclean, *A River Runs Through It,* 92.

108 Herrigel, *Zen in the Art of Archery,* 43. His book is a classic of Zen psychology and philosophy.

109 Camuto, *Hunting from Home,* 247.

110 Gill, *Bouldering,* 140–141. The rugged, competitive sport of bouldering can manifest an "inner" game similar in many respects to

the "inner" games of tennis, golf, chess, bridge, etc. The achievement of technical skill, whether kinesthetic or intellectual, can be ecstatic.

111 Hillman, *Blue Fire*, 180.

112 Ibid.

113 King, *Globalization and the Soul*, 28–30. Teilhard de Chardin is quoted in several of his writings. The Jesuit priest, mystic, and philosopher was profoundly affected by the violence, suffering and death he encountered during his wartime service.

114 *Bhagavad Gita*, 6:2 and 2:31.

115 Underhill, *Mysticism and War*, 25.

116 Cooper, *Playing the Zone*, 33.

117 See Murphy and White, *In the Zone*. The authors have assembled 1545 bibliographic entries in their 302-page book. These are catalogued into categories such as mystical sensations of detachment, floating, ecstasy, unity; altered perceptions of time, size, and light; out-of-body experiences; and extraordinary feats involving exceptional energy. The sheer volume of entries seems to have hampered their ability to unify mystical experiences in athletics to some common basis, a common problem when writing about any form of mysticism.

118 Cooper, *Playing the Zone*, 38.

119 Benson, *Timeless Healing*, 90. The Harvard physician also studied physiological reactions in mystics, including Hindu monks called *sanyasis*, and recorded remarkable changes during meditation. These are evidently controlled from the midbrain through blockage of afferent cortical pathways. Murphy and White, 138–148, have compared some of these physiological achievements with those of athletes.

120 Roger Bannister—later Sir Roger, then a medical student at Oxford—broke the four-minute barrier in the English mile run on May 6, 1954.

121 Ackerman, *Deep Play*, 194. Quoted from Robert Lipsyte, 1975. *Sportsword*. New York: Quadrangle Books. 280.

122 Andrews, *Psychic Power of Running*, 82–83. Valerie Andrews often quotes the psychiatrist Thaddeus Kostrubala (*The Joy of Running*, Philadelphia: Lippincott:1976), himself an avid runner who developed a clinic and psychotherapeutic program based on running. His concept of Paleoanalytic psychology is based on the idea that human beings' unique capacity and superiority in long distance running is the principal evolutionary step towards our present status and is recapitulated in embryogenesis. Our consciousness is a direct result of these evolutionary stages of running capacity according to Kostrubala.

123 Leo Tolstoy, *Anna Karenina* (London: Penguin, 1978 reprint).

124   Herzog, *Annapurna*, 16. Annapurna was the first peak over eight thousand meters in height to be climbed.

125   Muir, *The Wild Muir,* 92. Muir made the first ascent of Mount Ritter in the Sierra Nevada in 1872. As usual, he climbed alone and without any climbing paraphernalia.

126   Jenkins, *Perfume in the Ozone,* 29.

127   Hemingway, *Death in the Afternoon,* 216.

128   Crane, *Red Badge of Courage*, 116.

129   Austin, *Zen and the Brain,* 542. The neurologist James Austin wrote the monumental *Zen and the Brain* after experiencing an ecstasy in a grimy London Underground station on his way to a Zen Buddhist retreat. He stated, "I had a sense of eternity. My old yearnings, loathings, fear of death and insinuations of selfhood vanished. I had been graced by a comprehension of the ultimate nature of things." *Newsweek*, May 7, 2001, p. 50.

      Austin defines kensho (*ken-* seeing into something; *sho-* one's true nature) by 18 criteria among which William James's four criteria for mystical experience are essentially included. Noteworthy for the discussion on danger is the sense of release in which fear vanishes with a sense of total mental and physical relief.

130   Ibid., 148.

131   Shakespeare, *Hamlet*, Act III, Scene i, lines 85–90.

132   Todhunter, *Dangerous Games,* 71.

133   H. James, *Letters,* 2:76–77.

134   *Varieties*, 380–381.

135   Wittgenstein, *Tractatus*, 6.522.

136   Roth, *Original Tao*, 142–143. Nei-yeh comes from early Taoism (400 B.C.E.) and describes methods for mystical "inner cultivation."

137   Jeffries, *Story of My Heart,* 18.

138   Martin, *Does It Matter*, 23.

139   Ibid., 380.

140   Martin, 6. He cites Michael Polanyi, *The Tacit Dimension* (London, 1967), and constructs many of his ideas about mysticism from this seemingly simple insight.

141   Swedenborg, *Arcana Coelestia*, 5121.2–3.

142   Martin, *Shadows in the Cave,* 214. He quotes at length passages by Simon Leys in *The Burning Forest* (London, 1988) on the origin and concept of *qi.*

143   W. James, *Varieties*, 501.

144   Bergson, *Creative Evolution*, 291.

145   Ibid., 295.

146   W. James, in his lecture "On a Certain Blindness in Humanity" in *Talks to Teachers*, 855.

147 Austin, *Zen and the Brain*, 300–305.
148 Rolland, *Life of Ramakrishna*, 33.
149 For a discussion of the Freud-Rolland correspondence, see Parsons, *The Enigma of the Oceanic Feeling*.
150 Freud, *Civilization and its Discontents*, 770:

> Thus we are willing to acknowledge that the "oceanic" feeling exists in many people, and we are disposed to relate it to an early stage of ego-feeling; the further question arises: what claim has this feeling to be regarded as the source of the need for religion.
>
> To me this claim does not seem very forcible. Surely a feeling can only be a source of energy when it is itself the expression of a strong need. The derivation of a need for religion from a child's feeling of haplessness and the longing it evokes for a father seems to me incontrovertible, especially since this feeling is not simply carried on from childhood days but is kept perpetually alive by the fear of what superior power of fate will bring. I could not point to any need in childhood so strong as that for father's protection. Thus the part played by the "oceanic" feeling, which I suppose seeks to reinstate limitless narcissism, cannot possibly take the first place. The derivation of the religious attitude can be followed back in clear outline as far as the child's feeling of helplessness. There may be something else behind this, but for the present it is wrapped in obscurity.
>
> I can imagine that the "oceanic" feeling could become connected with religion later on. That feeling of oneness with the universe which in its ideational content sounds very like a first attempt at the consolation of religion, like another way taken by the ego of denying the dangers it sees threatening it in the external world. I must confess I find it very difficult to work with these intangible quantities. Another friend of mine whose insatiable scientific curiosity has impelled him to the most out-of-the-way researches and to the acquisition of encyclopedic knowledge, has assured me that the yogi by their practice of withdrawal from the world, concentrating attention on body functions, peculiar methods of breathing, actually are able to produce new sensations and diffused feeling in themselves which he regards as regressions to primordial, deeply buried mental states. He sees in them a physiological foundation, so to speak, of much of the wisdom of mysticism. There would be connections to be made here with many obscure modifications of mental life, such as trance and ecstasy. But I am moved to exclaim, in the words of Schiller's diver: "Who breathes overhead in the rose-tinted light may be glad!"

Anthony Storr discusses the conflict within Freud about the "oceanic" feeling and, in Storr's judgment, the error in Freud's reasoning that mystical states of mind are merely regressive and narcissistic. His book is, in addition, a splendidly written exploration of the connection between solitude and the creative personality. *Solitude,* 38–39.

For an exhaustive exploration of the "oceanic feeling," with a detailed analysis of the correspondence between Freud and Rolland, and numerous examples of nature ecstasies experienced by Rolland, see Parsons' *The Enigma of the Oceanic Feeling.*

151   See Sigmund Freud's letter to his friend Wilhelm Fliess regarding his struggle to write a "psychology for neurologists," in *Complete Psychological Works,* vol. 1, 283–285.

152   M. Csikszentmihalyi, *Flow: Psychology of Optimal Experience,* 251.

153   A prolific nature writer, Diane Ackerman has written a lyric description of her own mystic connection to nature (*Deep Play,* 13).

154   Herbert Benson has applied his studies to the counseling and treatment of patients at his clinic in Boston (*Break-out Principle,* 236).

155   Susan Greenwood's *The Nature of Magic: An Anthropology of Consciousness* is a compendium of experiences in various forms of nature or "Earth" religion, including paganism, Wicca, druidism, shamanism, and much dealing with New Age spirituality. She explains her philosophy particularly in the Introduction.

156   Eddington, *Nature of the Physical World,* 321.

157   Mercer, *Nature Mysticism,* 4. The book is a delightful and poetic source to which I bow. Mercer has this to say about the Almighty: "... let the name of God be reserved for the phenomenal aspect of the Absolute. But the nature-mystic will be wise if he discards compromise, and once for all repudiates the Unconditioned Absolute. His reason can then chime in with his intuitions and his deepest emotions. He loses nothing; he gains intellectual peace and natural joy."

158   Benson's book *Timeless Healing* discusses many of the remarkable psychic influences upon physiological responses as well as what may happen when psyches go awry.

159   Walsh, *Spirit of Shamanism,* 8.

160   The traditional healer, like his modern counterpart, is not always successful. My friend eventually had to have his misaligned fracture reset by an orthopedist.

161   Csikszentmihalyi, *Optimal Experience,* 33.

162   Walsh, *Spirit of Shamanism,* 262. The author reviews the old traditions and demonstrates how modern medicine may benefit. He invokes the need for solitude for psychological and spiritual development (52–55). See also "Solitude" in chapter 1 and Anthony Storr's *Solitude.*

163   See the following note. The word "sower" seems to be a mistake in translation that has been endlessly repeated. Einstein used "Quelle," which means "source" and has nothing to do with "sower."

164   The science writer John Horgan also used the term "rational mysticism" in his book of the same name. He focused upon chemical pathways and drug actions in reproducing mystical experience.

165   Jammer, *Einstein and Religion*, 126:

> When he [Einstein] was asked, early in 1921, whether he believed that the soul exists and continues to exist after death, he replied, "the mystical trend of our present time, showing itself especially in the exuberant growth of the so-called Theosophy and Spiritualism is for me only a symptom of weakness and confusion."

In 1955, he wrote, "What I see in nature is a magnificent structure that we can comprehend only imperfectly, and that must fill a thinking person with a feeling of 'humility.' This is a genuine religious feeling that has nothing to do with mysticism."

Janner, in trying to define Einstein's religious viewpoint, says, "If mysticism denotes immediate intuition of, or insight into, a spiritual truth in a way different from ordinary sense perception, or the use of logical thinking, Einstein was never a mystic."

I believe that the term "ordinary sense perception" is key to distinguishing Einstein's belief system from that which he considered mysticism. In our discussion of nature mysticism, there is no point of sense perception that exceeds the "normal," at least qualitatively. What mystical experience involves in this context is a vast expansion or enhancement of consciousness, which leads to the sublime and creative moments that have been called ecstatic.

166   The ultimate attribution of Einstein's statements that are discussed here has been difficult but fascinating. It is fairly certain that his original statement (version 1 in the following comparisons) was written in German about 1930, in a short paper, "Wie ich die Welt sehe," which was published in 1934 in *Mein Weltbild* (Frankfurt: Ullstein Materielien, 1980, 9–10). This was then translated into English in 1931 (Jammer, *Einstein and Religion*). Einstein then modified the statement for a phonograph recording in 1932 as part of his *Glaubensbekenntnis* (Credo), documented in Friedrich Herneck, 1976, *Einstein und sein Weltbild*. Berlin: Buchverlag der Morgen, 100–101 (version 2). Various English translations of this statement appear on the internet. The final version has been traced back as far as 1948 in *The Universe and Dr. Einstein* (New York: Sloan Associates). Lincoln Barnett, the author, introduces the aphorism

(on page 105) by writing, "Einstein, whose philosophy of science
has been sometimes been criticized as materialistic, once said: 'The
most beautiful and most profound emotion we can experience is the
sensation of the mystical....' " Barnett continues, "...and on another
occasion he (Einstein) declared, 'The cosmic religious experience
is the strongest and noblest mainspring of scientific research.' "
The author gives us no citation details. Thus we have a quotation
involving the word "mystical" that has been used hundreds if not
thousands of times (to judge from searching the internet), that
cannot be directly traced to Einstein's speeches or writings. The
only certainty of its veracity as a statement by Einstein is that he,
himself, wrote the foreword to Barnett's book. In order to trace the
progression of this statement from its origin, three versions in English
and the original German are compared in the table opposite.

167 Honner, "Niels Bohr and the Mysticism of Nature," in *Zygon*, 243.
168 The interview with Heisenberg was recorded in the chapter "A
Question of Physics" in *Conversations in Physics and Biology*, 3
(Toronto: University of Toronto Press, 1979).
169 Richard Lewontin in a book review, *New York Review of Books*,
October 20, 2005, p. 54.
170 Wilson, *Consilience*, 261.
171 P. V. Inayat Khan, 2001. From talks given on October 21–23 at
Harvard University (in *Spirit of Change: New England's Holistic
Magazine*, Sept.–Oct. 2002).
172 Russell, *Mysticism and Logic*, 12.
173 Newburg and d'Aquili, *Why God Won't Go Away*.
174 H. James, *Letters, v. II*, 149–150. To Henry W. Rankin, June 16,
1901. This often quoted letter summarizes the heart of James's
creation of *The Varieties of Religious Experience*.
175 W. James, "A Suggestion about Mysticism," 159.
176 W. James, *Varieties*, 377, in the introductory paragraph of the first
lecture (XVI) on mysticism.
177 H. James, *Letters of William James*, vol. 2, 210 (June 10, 1901).
178 Notes, p. 194, in *Essays in Philosophy*.
179 W. James, *Pluralistic Universe*, 289, 169.
180 Ibid., 150.
181 Donnelly, *Reinterpreting the Legacy of William James*. 259. In chapter
by Adler, Hulmut A., "William James and Gustav Fechner: From
Rejection to Elective Affinity."
182 Fechner, *Elemente der Psychophysik*, 530:

Hier stellen a, b, c drei Organismen oder vielmehr die psycho-
physishcen Hauptwellen dreier Organismen vor, AB die Schwelle.

VERSION 1 1930	VERSION 2 1932	VERSION 3 PRE-1948
The most beautiful experience we can have is the mysterious.	The most beautiful and most profound that a person can experience is the mysterious.	The most beautiful and most profound emotion we can experience is the mystical.
It is the fundamental emotion, which stands at the cradle of true art and true science.	It is the foundation of religion as well as deeper strivings of art and science.	It is the sower* of all true science. *Source = *quelle*
Whoever does not know it and can no longer wonder, no longer marvel, is as good as dead, and his eyes are dimmed.	Who never experienced that seems to me if not a dead person but then a blind person.	He to whom this emotion is a stranger, who can no longer wonder and stand rapt in awe, is as good as dead.
Das Schönste was wir erleben können, ist das Geheimnissvolle.	Das schönste und tiefste, was der Mensch erlben kann, ist das Gefühl des Geheimnissvollen.	Das schönste und tiefste Gefühl, was wir erleben können, ist die Empfindung des Mystischen.
Es ist das Grundegefühl, das der Wiege von wahrer Kunst und Wissenschaft steht.	Es liegt der Religion sowie allem tieferen Strebe in Kunst und Wissenschaft zugrunde.	Es ist Quelle aller wahren Wissenschaft.
Wer es nicht kennt und sich nicht mehr wundern, nicht mehr staunen kann, der is sozusagen tot und sein Auge erloschen.	Wer dies nicht erlebt hat, erscheint mir, wenn nicht wie ein Toter, so doch ein Blinder.	Wem dieses Gefühl fremd ist, wer nicht mehr staunen und nicht mehr in Ehrfurcht versinken kann, der ist so gut wie tot.

> Was von jedem Wellenberge die Schwelle überragt, hängt in sich zusammen und trägt ein einiges Bewusstsein; was unter der Schwelle ist, trennt als Unbewusstsein tragend das Bewusste, indess es doch noch die physische Verbindung dazwischen unterhält.

In his copy (now at the Houghton Library), William James has underlined several phrases of Fechner's wave concept. In his *Human Immortality* (p. 59), he translates it thus:

> In this figure a, b, c stand for three organisms, or rather for the total waves of psycho-physical activity of three organisms, whilst AB represents the threshold. In each wave the part that rises above the threshold is an integrated thing, and is connected with a single consciousness. Whatever lies below the threshold, being unconscious, separates the conscious crests, although it is still the means of physical connection.

183   William James, in note 6 of his Ingersoll Lecture on "Human Immortality," comments:

> One easily sees how, on Fechner's wave-scheme, a world-soul may be expressed. All psychophysical activity being continuous "below the threshold," the consciousness might also be continuous if the threshold sank low enough to uncover all the waves. The threshold throughout nature in general is, however, very high, so the consciousness that gets over it is of the discontinuous form.

184   William James invokes the oceanic and tidal metaphor in several of his works. In "A Suggestion about Mysticism" (157–158), he presents his concept of Fechner's wave-scheme:

> The suggestion, stated very briefly, is that states of mystical intuition may be only very sudden and great extensions of the ordinary "field of consciousness." Concerning the causes of such extensions I have no suggestions to make; but the extension itself would, if my view is correct, consist in an immense spreading of the margin of the field, so that knowledge ordinarily transmarginal would become included, and the ordinary margin would grow more central. Fechner's "wave-scheme" will diagram the alteration, as I conceive it, if we suppose that the wave of present awareness, steep above the horizontal line that represents the plane of the usual "threshold," slopes away below it very gradually in all directions. A fall of the threshold, however caused, would, under these circumstances, produce the state of things, which we see on an unusually

flat shore at the ebb of the spring tide. Vast tracts usually covered are then revealed to view, but nothing rises more than a few inches above the water's bed, and great parts of the scene are submerged again whenever a wave washes over them.

In another example, in *Human Immortality*:

According to the state in which the brain finds itself, the barrier of its obstructiveness may also be supposed to rise or fall. It sinks so low, when the brain is in full activity that a comparative flood of spiritual energy pours in. At other times, only such occasional waves of thought as heavy sleep permits get by. (17)

James regarded the theory of "threshold of consciousness" with deepest confidence and of great importance to psychology (Bush, *William James and Panpsychism,* 322). A poetic New England metaphor of James is seen in *Memories and Studies,* 204:

Out of my experience...one fixed conclusion dogmatically emerges... that we with our lives are like islands in the sea or trees in the forest. The maple and pine may whisper to each other with their leaves. And Conanicut and Newport hear each other's foghorns. But the trees commingle their roots in the darkness under ground and the islands also hang together through the ocean bottom. Just so there is a continuity of cosmic consciousness against which several minds plunge as into a Mother Sea or reservoir.... What are the conditions of individuation or insulation in this mother-sea? We need only suppose the continuity of our unconscious with a mother-sea, to allow waves pouring over the dam. Of course these odd lowerings of the brain's threshold remain a mystery on any terms.

185   W. James, "A Suggestion about Mysticism," 158. James concludes this essay:

I have treated the phenomenon under discussion as if it uncovered tracts of *consciousness.* Is the consciousness already there waiting to be uncovered? And is it veridical revelation of reality? These are question on which I do not touch. In the subjects of the experience the "emotion of conviction" is always strong, and sometimes absolute. The ordinary psychologist disposes of the phenomenon under the conveniently "scientific" head of *petit mal,* if not "bosh" or "rubbish." But we know so little of the noetic value of abnormal mental states of any kind that in my opinion we had better keep an open mind and collect facts sympathetically for a long time to come. We shall not *understand* these alterations of consciousness either in this generation or in the next.

How prescient he was!

186   Peirce, *Collected Papers*, vol. 7, para. 547.

187   Restak, *Mysteries of the Mind*, 77.

188   Ibid., 86. Restak cites the work of Robert Pollack, who adds:

> This wave links the centers responsible for processing sensory information to one another as well as to other centers responsible for unconscious and conscious activities of the mind, in particular the amygdala, the hippocampus, and the frontal cortex, where, broadly speaking, emotional states are generated, long-term memories stored, and the intentions to speak and act generated.

189   Zohar and Marshall, *Spiritual Intelligence,* 62–63. The author presents her concepts of *SQ,* spiritual intelligence, which in large part embraces my concepts of mysticism, broadly as they may be painted. Conversely, my thoughts can be largely translated into "spiritual intelligence."

190   Austin, *Zen and the Brain,* 298.

191   W. James, *Principles,* 219–278.

192   Ibid., 272–273. James may have studied analytic geometry in his intense, mostly European education, but expressed the concept of this fairly sophisticated mathematical model in terms easily grasped by the general reader. This is just a further example of the clearness and accessibility of his thinking and writing. Diagrammatic models did fascinate him, and as we will see, influenced much of his visual thinking about the "mother sea of consciousness" and Fechner's wave theory.

193   Ibid., 272.

194   Bohm, *Thought as a System.* 131–134.

195   W. James, *Pluralistic Universe*, 231–2. James considered the threshold of Fechner "as only one way of naming the quantitative discreteness in the change of all our sensible experience."

196   A. Huxley, *Heaven and Hell,* 155.

197   Herbert Benson described the scientific basis for the relaxation response in his chapter in *Encyclopedia of Neuroscience*, vol. 2 (Boston: Birkhäuser, 1987,1043–1047).

198   Zaehner, *Mysticism Sacred and Profane*, xii–xiii.

199   Vaitl et al., *Psychobiology of Altered States of Consciousness.*

200 Leuba, *Psychology of Religious Mysticism*, 255ff. "Few of the lesser trance-phenomena are more striking and incontestably wholly physiological in origin than a peculiar appearance of light or brilliance which may be called photism. Mystics frequently use the word 'light,' but it is not always possible to know whether they use it in a symbolical or in a realistic sense. In a great number of instances, however, the perceptual quality of the experience cannot be doubted."

201 Wordsworth, *Essential Wordsworth,* from *The Prelude,* "I walked with nature," lines 16–18.

202 Alcoholics Anonymous, *"Pass It On,"* 121.

203 Dean, *Psychiatry and Mysticism,* 10.

204 G. Taylor, *Natural History of the Mind,* 111. Taylor describes some experiments in meditation: "—we see regression to Phase Two (paleomammalian or midbrain function) before our very eyes; colors become more vivid,—which I interpret as the breakdown of cortically mediated vision in favor of thalamic vision." This entire chapter on unusual states of consciousness is well worth reading for the interested.

205 Austin, *Zen and the Brain*, 241.

206 Hunt, *On the Nature of Consciousness,* 156–159.

207 Ibid., 105.

208 Helen Phillips, "The Genius Machine," *New Scientist,* April 2, 2004, 30–33.

209 Mandell, *Toward a Psychobiology of Transcendence,* 393, 438.

210 Pert, *Molecules of Emotion,* 133.

211 Goldstein uses the word "thrill" to convey the emotions of hearing music. That word can fit into my broad glossary of synonyms for mystical experience. His study upon student volunteers is quoted by Levinthal, *Messengers of Paradise,* 178–179.

212 d'Aquili and Newberg, *Religious and Mystical States*, 185.

213 Manisha Roy, personal communication.

214 *Apophasis* has several meanings, but when used in a philosophical or religious sense it is a negation or emptying out (from the Greek "to deny" or "to say no"), as in so-called negative or *apophatic* theology, which relates to the *via negativa* of ancient philosophy. A related expression, *exinanition*, often referring to Jesus's crucifixion, means an emptying out of the spirit, desolation, enfeeblement, or exhaustion. The distinction I seek to show is the positive spiritual action of emptying out the mind, at least temporarily, of the cobwebs and dust of the cerebral noise that besets us all in daily life.

215 Roth, *Original Tao*, 126.

216 Peat, *The Blackwinged Night,* 96. David Peat translates quantum theory for the ordinary reader like myself and takes us on a roller

coaster ride to show how such incredible energy can exist in the *plenum* of the vacuum state. He proceeds (p. 91) to draw parallels with the void that I describe of mystic consciousness.

> The total absence—the negation that, at the same time, is a plenum and absolute fullness—is found in the writings of mystics. It is also the vision expressed by artists and musicians alike. All that exists outside the void and in the domain of time is, to some extent, conditioned. For the Buddhist and physicist alike, to be tied to the wheel of time is to be caught up in the eternal web of cause and effect. The void, the negation of all, lies beyond this causality. It is unconditioned, pure potential.

217   Forman, *Mysticism, Mind, Consciousness,* 171–172.
218   Stace, *Mysticism and Philosophy,* 162ff.
219   *Arcana Coelestia,* 1937.
220   d'Aquili and Newberg, *Religious and Mystical States,* 185.
221   W. James, *Varieties,* 394.
222   New York: Doubleday, 2004.
223   W. James. *Varieties,* 37–38.
224   Leary, *The Politics of Ecstasy,* 1965.
225   Barnard, *Exploring Unseen Worlds,* 25–26. He discusses James's experiments at length and concludes:

> This account of James's experiment gives us a glimpse of the strength of James's character. We see here not only James's courageous receptivity to the unknown and the unconventional (as well as his openness to ideas that would reverse years of personal philosophical work), but also his willingness to share this unorthodox experience with his academic colleagues. Further, James's comments on his nitrous oxide experience are also an immensely fertile source of insights into the roots of James's later, more developed philosophical stance on mysticism. To begin with, this account is a clear demonstration of his methodology: phenomenological reporting first, followed by an intellectual and ethical assessment. We can see also evidence of James's later stress on the emotional aspects of mystical experience, as well as the characteristics of ineffability, noetic quality, transciency and inner unity that James repeatedly associates with mystical experience in his later philosophy of mysticism. Finally, this account also illustrates the ways in which James's repeated emphasis on the theme of reconciliation in philosophical work—the reconciliation between self and God that is stressed in *The Varieties,* as well as the reconciliation between

mind and matter that was attempted in his later radical empiricism—is intimately connected with his understanding of mystical experience.

226 These comments are quoted by Zaehner, *Mysticism Sacred and Profane,* 114–116. Health guru Andrew Weil, who publishes the circular *Self Healing,* in his book *The Natural Mind* advocates drugs as a tool to enter other states of consciousness (pp. 194–195).

227 Laski, *Ecstasy,* 43.

228 There is a dampening of the dopamine reward circuitry when extrinsic drugs of abuse are administered, which increases tolerance and thus increased and repeated demand for the drug. See "The Addicted Brain" by neuropharmacologists Eric J. Nestler and Robert C. Malencka in *Scientific American,* March 2004, 78–85.

229 Ibid., 83.

230 *Tikkun* Jan.–Feb. 2004.

231 Raine, *House of the Soul,* 263.

232 W. Stevens, *Wallace Stevens,* 929–930.

233 Burke, *Sublime and Beautiful,* 57.

234 Ibid., 73.

235 Myers, *Wordsworth,* 130.

236 J. Huxley, *New Bottles for New Wine,* 311. "In the light of evolutionary humanism, however, the connection became clear, though the intellectual formulation given by Wordsworth was inadequate. The reality behind his thought is that man's mind is a partner with nature: it participates with the external world in the process of generating awareness and creating values." Elsewhere in his chapter titled "Evolutionary Humanism" Huxley states,

> I submit that the discoveries of physiology, general biology, and psychology not only make possible, but necessary, a naturalistic hypothesis, in which there is no room for the supernatural, and the spiritual forces at work in the cosmos are seen as part of nature just as much as the material forces. What is more, these spiritual forces are one particular product of mental activity in the broad sense, and mental activities in general are seen to be increased in intensity and importance during the course of cosmic time. Our basic hypothesis is thus not merely naturalistic as opposed to supernaturalistic, but monistic or unitary as opposed to dualistic, and evolutionary, as opposed to static. (286)

Note well that Huxley nowhere specifies mental activity to be solely human.

237 A. Huxley, *Wordsworth in the Tropics,* 334–341.

238 De Quincey, *De Quincey as Critic,* 442. Thomas De Quincey was a good friend of Wordsworth and often took long walks with him. He describes the following incident while they were waiting for an overdue mail carriage around midnight:

> At intervals, Wordsworth had stretched himself at length on the high road, applying his ear to the ground, so as to catch any sound of wheels that might be groaning in the distance. Once, when he was slowly rising from his effort, his eye caught a bright star that was glittering between the brow of Seat Sandal, and of the mighty Helvellyn. He gazed upon it for a minute or so; and then turning away to descend into Grasmere, he made the following explanation. [the quotation then follows]

239 Stallknecht, *Strange Seas of Thought,* 101ff.

240 Ibid., 12. There seems to be much that connects Wordsworth with William James. In several of his passages Wordsworth's pragmatic approach to underlying consciousness recalls James's conceptual constructions discussed in chapter 6.

241 Myers, *Wordsworth,* 137.

242 Hodder, *Thoreau's Ecstatic Witness,* 60–61.

243 Emerson, *Nature,* 88.

244 Richardson, *Emerson,* 548.

245 Thoreau, *Journal,* 1:74–75. March 3, 1839. It can be seen why some ecogenderists are incensed by Thoreau's "sexist" literary style.

246 Thoreau, *Collected Poems,* 230–231.

247 Elder, *Imagining the Earth,* 215.

248 Slovik, *Seeking Awareness in American Nature Writing,* 76.

249 Ann Skea has published a well-thought-out paper on "Ted Hughes and the British Bardic Tradition" on the internet.

250 Gifford, *Green Voices,* 134. "Green poetry" is a step further than nature poetry; the poet is not just an observer but is directly engaged in environmental issues. The poetry of Ted Hughes is considered "the most daring and comprehensive" attempt to explore the processes that involve the natural world.

251 In *Ted Hughes: Collected Poems,* edited by Paul Keegan (New York: Farrar, Straus, & Giroux: 2003), p. 660.

252 Ibid., 1214–1215.

253 Ibid., 675.

254 Barbara Hurd, *Entering the Stone: On Caves and Feeling Through the Dark* (Boston: Houghton Mifflin, 2003).

255 Martin, *Shadows in the Cave,* 204.

256 David Bohm, quoted by Dunstan Martin, 120.

257 Lewis-Williams, 2002, *The Mind in the Cave.* In a well-illustrated book, the author presents his theories behind prehistoric art. As others have asserted, he believes that shamanistic practice and primitive spiritualism were the factors leading to the burst of creative energy in Upper Paleolithic humankind. The mystic connection of ancient humanity to its environment, increasingly masked by "rational" consciousness, survives and warrants nurture.

258 See Griffin, *Animal Thinking,* for examples of intelligent behavior throughout the animal world that equate to conscious thinking.

259 Martin, *Shadows in the Cave,* 204.

260 See Service and Bradley, *Megaliths,* for a survey of these giant rock installations, particularly in Europe.

261 Emerson, *Nature*, 38.

262 Rowley, *Chinese Painting*, 20.

263 See Mowry, *Worlds Within Worlds,* for a splendid pictorial essay on Chinese scholars' rocks.

264 Hay, *Kernels of Energy, Bones of Earth,* 144. The garden and rock were objects of Chinese art connoisseurs' admiration of nature as a thing in itself. Hay presents the history of many classical representations of the rock in Chinese art.

265 Rosenblum, *Art of the Natural World,* 39.

266 Coupe, *Green Studies Reader,* 223–226. In the chapter by B. and T. Roszak, "Deep Form in Art and Nature."

267 Taylor, Richard B. "Order in Pollock's Chaos," in *Scientific American,* December 2002, 116–121.

268 Emerson, *Journals,* 5: 137.

269 PBS, October 1998.

270 Subsequently, after painstaking reevaluation, Wiles concluded that there might be no solution to Fermat's mysterious theorem. The mathematical community, however, now widely accepts Wiles's proof.

271 Alan Lightman considered that ecstatic moment as a central one in his life. It conforms to a mystic state as defined by the criteria that William James applied. *A Sense of the Mysterious* (New York: Pantheon, 2005, pp. 16–17).

272 Nietzsche, *Ecce Homo,* 300. This section of his description of writing *Thus Spoke Zarathustra* stands as a memorable contribution to the creative experience.

273 Leuba, *The Psychology of Religious Mysticism,* 242.

274 Ibid., 240. The citation from Goethe is in Ackerman's *Gespräche mit Goethe,* v. 3: 166–7, Leipzig: Moldenhauer.

275 Thoreau, Entry of August 13, 1838 in *Journal,* v. 1, 50–51.

276 Greeley, *Ecstasy: A Way of Knowing.* He cites several sources in literature and science in order to support his thesis that ecstasy is a "dramatically different form of cognition."

277 Wilson, *Consilience*, 282.

278 Barg, Marianne. *CNN News.* http://www.cnn.com/2000/world/asiapcf/south08/42/asia.haze.

279 Wilson, *Future of Life*, 58.

280 Al Gore developed his crusade of many years into *An Inconvenient Truth: The Planetary Emerging Global Warming and What We Can Do about It* (Emmaus: Pennsylvania: Rodale Press) and the film with the same title.

281 Sinnot, *Bridge of Life*, 12.

282 von Wright, *Vetenskapen och förnuftet.* This book is based upon his lecture "Images of Science and Forms of Rationality," given at a colloquium by the European Science Foundation in Colmar, April 1985. Wright (deceased in 2003) was a successor to Wittgenstein as Professor of Philosophy at Cambridge University and was Emeritus Professor at Helsingfors University.

283 Suzuki, *Sacred Balance*, 174.

284 Bookchin, *Organic Society,* 66.

285 Ibid., 71.

286 Polanyi, *Tacit Dimension,* 92.

287 See Bill Moyer's discussion of the political and ecological implication of fundamentalist beliefs in the Rapture. *The New York Review of Books,* "Welcome to Doomsday," March 21, 2004, 8–10.

288 Naess, *Life's Philosophy,* 100. He writes: "Human beings do not have the right to reduce the richness and diversity of life...."

289 Roszak, *Voice of the Earth*, 252.

290 Milton, *Loving Nature*, 75.

291 Ibid., 199.

292 Stephen Jay Gould, *Natural History*, Sept. 1991, p. 14.

293 Abram, *Spell of the Sensuous*, 69.

294 An interview with George Schaller in *National Geographic Magazine*, October 2006. He went on to say, "You can't buy spiritual values at a shopping mall. The things that uplift the spirit—an old-growth forest, a clear river, the flight of a golden eagle, the howl of a wolf, space and quiet without motors—are intangible. These are the values that people do look for and that everyone needs."

295 Kellert, *Kinship and Mastery.* 205.

296 Hoffman, *Visions of Innocence*, 34.

297 Ibid., 39.

298 Ibid., 43.

299   de Duve, *Life Evolving*, vii.

300   Richard Louv, *Last Child in the Woods*.

301   Wells, Nancy M. and Kristi S. Lekies, "Nature and the Life
Course: Pathways from Childhood Nature Experiences to Adult
Environmentalism," in *Children, Youth and Environment* 16(1), 2006,
pp. 1–24.

302   Chawla, *Ecstatic Places*, 22.

303   Kaplan, *Experience of Nature*, 147.

304   Wordsworth, *Preface to Lyrical Ballads*, 1800, para. 9, line 13.

305   The writer and zoologist Matt Ridley documents the best and worst
sides of human instincts in *The Origins of Virtue: Human Instincts and
the Evolution of Cooperation* (New York: Penguin 1996, p. 264).

306   Stephanie Mills writes an impassioned chapter, "The Wild and the
Tame," in Burks, *Place of the Wild*, 45.

307   Theodore Roszak presents a historical and analytic discussion of
ecofeminism in *Voice of the Earth*, 233–246.

308   Buell, *Environmental Imagination*, 2.

309   Thomashow, *Bringing the Biosphere Home*, 192.

310   W. James. *Varieties*, 367.

311   *Bhagavad Gita*, 15:4.

Reference List

Abram, David. 1996. *The Spell of the Sensuous: Perception and Language in a More-Than-Human World*. New York: Pantheon.

Ackerman, Diane. 1999. *Deep Play*. New York: Random House.

Adams, Cass. 1996. *The Soul Unearthed: Celebrating Wildness and Personal Renewal through Nature*. New York: Jeremy P. Tarcher/Putnam.

Alcoholics Anonymous. 1984. *"Pass It On": The Story of Bill Wilson and How the A.A. Message Reached the World*. New York: Alcoholics Anonymous World Services.

Alter, Stephen. 2001. *Sacred Waters: a Pilgrimage Up the Ganges River to The Source of Hindu Culture*. New York: Harcourt.

Andrews, Valerie. 1978. *The Psychic Power of Running: How the Body Can Illuminate the Mysteries of the Mind*. New York: Rawson, Wade.

Austin, James. H. 1998. *Zen and the Brain: Toward an Understanding of Meditation and Consciousness*. Cambridge, MA: MIT Press.

Bannister, Roger. 1955. *The Four-Minute Mile*. New York: Dodd Mead.

Barnard, G. William. 1997. *Exploring Unseen Worlds: William James and the Philosophy of Mysticism*. Albany: State Univ. of New York Press.

Bergson, Henri. (1911) 1954. *Creative Evolution*. London: Macmillan.

Benson, Herbert. 1996. *Timeless Healing: The Power and Biology of Belief*. New York: Scribner.

———. 2003. *The Break-out Principle*. New York: Scribner.

Berry, Thomas. 1988. *The Dream of the Earth*. San Francisco: Sierra Club.

Beston, Henry. (1928) 1949. *The Outermost House: A Year of Life on the Great Beach of Cape Cod*. New York: Viking.

Bhagavad-Gita, The. 1986. Translated by Barbara Stoler Miller. New York: Bantam Dell.

Binet, Alfred. 1897. *The Psychic Life of Micro-Organisms: A Study in Experimental Psychology*. Chicago: Open Court.

Bloom, Howard. 2000. *Global Brain: The Evolution of Mass Mind from the Big Bang to the 21st Century*. New York: John Wiley.

Bohm, David. 1992. *Thought as a System*. London: Routledge.

Bookchin, Murray. 1997. "Organic Society." In *The Murray Bookchin Reader*. London: Cassell.

Bortoft, Henri. 1997. *The Wholeness of Nature: Goethe's Way toward a Science of Conscious Participation in Nature.* Great Barrington, MA: Lindisfarne Books.

Boulter, Michael. 2002. *Extinction: Evolution and the End of Man.* New York: Columbia University Press.

Brockington, A. Allen. 1934. *Mysticism and Poetry: On a Basis of Experience.* London: Chapman & Hall.

Bucke, Richard Maurice. 1901. *Cosmic Consciousness: A Study in the Evolution of the Human Mind.* Repr., New York: Dutton, 1970.

Buell, Lawrence. 1995. *The Environmental Imagination: Thoreau, Nature Writing, and the Formation of American Culture.* Cambridge, MA: Belknap Press of Harvard University Press.

———. 2001. *Writing for an Endangered World: Literature, Culture, and Environment in the U.S. and Beyond.* Cambridge, MA: Harvard University Press.

Burke, Edmund. (1757) 1958. *A Philosophical Enquiry into the Origin of Our Ideas of the Sublime and Beautiful.* London: Routledge and Kegan Paul.

Burks, David Clarke, ed. 1994. *Place of the Wild: A Wildlands Anthology.* Washington, DC: Island Press.

Bush, Wendell T. 1925. "William James and Panpsychism." In vol. 2 of *Studies in the History of Ideas.* New York: Columbia University Press.

Camuto, Christopher. 2003. *Hunting from Home: A Year Afield in the Blue Ridge Mountains.* New York: Norton.

Cardena, Etzel, Steven J. Lynn, and Stanley C. Kyppner, eds. 2000. *Varieties of Anomalous Experience: Examining the Scientific Evidence.* Washington, DC: American Psychological Association.

Cartmill, Matt. 1993. *A View to a Death in the Morning: Hunting and Nature through History.* Cambridge, MA: Harvard University Press.

Changeux, Jean-Pierre, and Jean Chavaillon, eds. 1995. *Origins of the Human Brain.* A Fyssen Foundation Symposium. Oxford: Clarendon Press.

Chawla, Louse. 1990. "Ecstatic Places." In *Children's Environments Quarterly,* 7 (4): 18–23.

Cooper, Andrew. 1998. *Playing in the Zone: Exploring the Spiritual Dimensions of Sports.* Boston: Shambala.

Corbett, Jim. 1953. *Jungle Lore.* New York: Oxford University Press.

Coupe, Laurence, ed. 2000. *The Green Studies Reader: From Romanticism to Ecocriticism.* London: Routledge.

Crane, Stephen. (1895) 1983. *The Red Badge of Courage: An Episode of the American Civil War.* New York: Penguin.

Crary, Jonathan. 1992. *Techniques of the Observer: On Vision and Modernity in the Nineteenth Century.* Cambridge, MA: MIT Press.

Csikszentmihalyi, Mihaly. 1979. *Finding Flow: The Psychology of Engagement with Everyday Life.* New York: Basic Books.

———. 1990. *Flow: The Psychology of Optimal Experience.* New York: Harper & Row.

———, and Isabella S. Csikszentmihalyi. 1988. *Optimal Experience: Psychological Studies of Flow in Consciousness.* Cambridge: Cambridge Univ. Press.

d'Aquili, Eugene, and Andrew B. Newberg. 1993. "Religious and Mystical States: A Neuropsychological Model. *Zygon: Journal of Religion and Science* 28 (June): 117–200.

———. 1999. *The Mystical Mind: Probing the Biology of Religious Experience.* Minneapolis: Fortress Press.

Darwin, Charles. (1844) 1989. *The Power of Movement in Plants.* New York: New York University Press.

———. (1859) 1988. *On the Origin of Species.* Works of Charles Darwin, vol. 15. London: Pickering.

Dean, Stanley R., ed. 1975. *Psychiatry and Mysticism.* Chicago: Nelson-Hall.

de Duve, Christian. 1995. *Vital Dust: Life as a Cosmic Imperative.* New York: Basic Books.

———. 2002. *Life Evolving: Molecules, Mind, and Meaning.* New York: Oxford University Press.

De Quincey, Thomas. 1973. *De Quincey as Critic.* Edited by John E. Jordan. London: Routledge.

Devereux, Paul. 2000. *The Sacred Place: The Ancient Origin of Holy and Mystical Sites.* London: Cassel & Co.

Dillard, Annie. 1974. *Pilgrim at Tinker Creek.* New York: Harper & Row, Perennial Library.

———. 1986. *Tickets for a Prayer Wheel.* New York: Harper & Row.

Donnelly, Margaret E., ed. *Reinterpreting the Legacy of William James.* Washington, DC: American Psychological Association.

Eddington, Arthur S. 1928. *The Nature of the Physical World.* New York: Macmillan.

———. 1929. *Science and the Unseen World.* New York: Macmillan.

Elvee, Richard Q., ed. 1981. *Mind in Nature: Nobel Conference XVII.* Gustavus Adolphus College. San Francisco: Harper & Row.

Emerson, Ralph Waldo. 1836. *Nature.* Boston: James Munroe.

———. (1844) 1971. *Nature,* in *Emerson's Essays,* introduction by Sherman Paul. Everyman's Library. New York: Dutton.

———. 1903. *The Complete Works of Ralph Waldo Emerson.* Edited by Edward Waldo Emerson. 14 vols. Boston: Houghton, Mifflin.

———. 1960–1982. *The Journals and Miscellaneous Notebooks of Ralph Waldo Emerson.* Edited by William H. Gilman et al. 16 vols. Cambridge, MA: Harvard University Press.

Fechner, Gustav Theodor. 1860. *Elemente der Psychophysik*, vol. 2. Leipzig: Breitkopf u. Härtel.

———. 1946. *Religion of a Scientist*. Selections from Gustav Theodor Fechner. Edited and translated by Walter Lowrie. New York: Pantheon.

Forman, Robert K. C. 1999. *Mysticism, Mind, Consciousness*. Albany: State University of New York Press.

Freud, Sigmund. 1957. *The Standard Edition of the Complete Psychological Works of Sigmund Freud*. Edited by James Strachey. London: Hogarth Press.

———. (1930) 1989. *Civilization and its Discontents*. Translated and edited by James Strachey. Standard ed. New York: Norton.

Gifford, Terry. 1995. *Green Voices: Understanding Contemporary Nature Poetry*. Manchester: Manchester University Press.

Gill, John. 1980. "Bouldering: a Mystic Art Form." In *The Mountain Spirit*, edited by M.C. Tobias and Harold Drasdo. London: Victor Gollanz.

Gore, Al. 1992. *Earth in the Balance: Ecology and the Human Spirit*. Boston: Houghton-Mifflin.

Gottlieb, Roger S., ed. 1996. *This Sacred Earth: Religion, Nature, Environment*. New York: Routledge.

Greeley, A. M. 1974. *Ecstasy: A Way of Knowing*. Englewood Cliffs, New Jersey: Prentice Hall.

———, and William McCready. "Are We a Nation of Mystics?" *New York Times Magazine,* January 16, 1975.

Greenwood, Susan. 2005. *The Nature of Magic: An Anthropology of Consciousness*. Oxford: Berg.

Griffin, Donald R. 1992. *Animal Minds*. Chicago: University of Chicago Press.

Haldane, J. B. S. 1985. *On Being the Right Size and Other Essays*. Oxford: Oxford University Press.

Hamer, Dean. 2004. *The God Gene: How Faith Is Hardwired into Our Genes*. New York: Doubleday.

Hay, John. 1985 (b.1939). *Kernels of Energy, Bones of Earth: The Rock in Chinese Art*. New York: China Institute of America.

Hay, John. 2004 (b.1915). *Mind the Gap: the Education of a Nature Writer*. Reno: University of Nevada Press.

Hemingway, Ernest. 1932. *Death in the Afternoon*. New York: Scribner.

Herrigel, Eugen. 1964. *Zen in the Art of Archery*. New York: Pantheon.

Herzog, Maurice. 1953. *Annapurna*. New York: E. P. Dutton.

Hillman, James. 1991. *A Blue Fire*. Selected writings by James Hillman introduced and edited by Thomas Moore. New York: Harper Perennial.

Hobson, J. Allan. 1999. *Consciousness.* New York: Scientific American Library.

Hodder, Alan. D. 2001. *Thoreau's Ecstatic Witness.* New Haven: Yale University Press.

Hoffman, Edward. 1992. *Visions of Innocence: Spiritual and Inspirational Experiences of Childhood.* Boston: Shambala.

Hofman, Albert. 1986. *Insight Outlook.* Atlanta, Georgia: Humanities New Age Press.

Honner, John. 1982. "Niels Bohr and the Mysticism of Nature." *Zygon: Journal of Religion and Science.* 17 (September) 243–253.

Horgan, John. 2002. *Rational Mysticism: Dispatches from the Border between Science and Spirituality.* Boston: Houghton Mifflin.

Hudson, W. H. (1918) 1997. *Far Away and Long Ago.* Introduction by Stephen J. Bodio. New York: Lyons and Burford.

Hughes. Ted. 1984. *River.* New York: Harper & Row.

Hunt, Harry T. 1995. *On the Nature of Consciousness: Cognitive, Phenomenological, and Transpersonal Perspectives.* New Haven: Yale University Press.

Huxley, Aldous. (1929) 2000. "Wordsworth in the Tropics." In *Complete Essays*, vol. 2: 1926–1929, pp. 334–341. (Originally in *Do What You Will.* London: Chatto and Windus, 1929). Chicago: Ivan R Dee.

———. (1956) 1963. *The Doors Of Perception and Heaven and Hell.* New York: Perennial Library.

Huxley, Julian. 1957. *New Bottles for New Wine.* New York: Harper.

Hvolbeck, Russell H. 1998. *Mysticism and Experience.* Lanham, MD: University Press of America .

James, Henry, ed. 1920. *The Letters of William James.* 2 vols. Boston: Atlantic Monthly Press.

James, William. (1890) 1983. *The Principles of Psychology.* 1890. Cambridge, MA: Harvard University Press.

———. (1899) 1983. *Talks to Teachers on Psychology: And to Students on Some of Life's Ideals.* Cambridge, MA: Harvard University Press.

———. 1902. *The Varieties of Religious Experience: A Study in Human Nature, Being the Gifford Lectures on Natural Religion Delivered at Edinburgh in 1901–1902.* New York: Longmans, Green.

———. (1909) 1996. *A Pluralistic Universe: Hibbert Lectures at Manchester College on the Present Situation in Philosophy.* Lincoln, NE: University of Nebraska Press.

———. (1910) 1978. "A Suggestion about Mysticism." In *Essays in Philosophy.* Cambridge: Harvard University Press.

———. (1911) 1968. *Memories and Studies.* New York: Greenwood Press.

————. 1976. *The Will to Believe and Other Essays in Popular Philosophy; Human Immortality, Two Supposed Objections to the Doctrine.* New York: Dover.

Jammer, Max. 1999. *Einstein and Religion: Physics and Theology.* Princeton, NJ: Princeton University Press.

Jeffries, Richard. 1947. *The Story of my Heart.* London: Constable.

Jenkins, Thomas M. 1979. "Perfume in the Ozone." *Summit,* June–July, 29.

Jonsson, Erik. 2002. *Inner Navigation: Why We Get Lost and How We Find Our Way.* New York: Scribner.

Jung, C. G. 1960. *The Collected Works of C. G. Jung.* Edited by Herbert Read et al. Princeton, NJ: Princeton University Press.

Kahn, Peter H. 1999. *The Human Relationship with Nature: Development and Culture.* Cambridge, MA.: MIT Press.

————, and Stephen R. Kellert. 2002. *Children and Nature: Psychological, Sociocultural, and Evolutionary Investigations.* Cambridge, MA: MIT Press.

Kaplan, R., and S. Kaplan. 1989. *The Experience of Nature: A Psychological Perspective.* New York: Cambridge University Press.

Kellert, Stephen R. 1997. *Kinship to Mastery: Biophilia in Human Evolution and Development.* Washington, DC: Island Press.

————, and Timothy J. Farnham, ed. 2002. *The Good in Nature and Humanity: Connecting Science, Religion, and Spirituality in the Natural World.* Washington, DC: Island Press.

————, and E. O. Wilson. 1993. *The Biophilia Hypothesis.* Washington, DC: Island Press.

Kelly, Kevin W. 1988. *The Home Planet.* Reading, MA: Addison-Wesley.

King, Thomas M. 2002. "Globalization and the Soul: According to Teilhard, Friedman and Others." *Zygon: Journal of Religion and Science.* 37 (March): 26–43.

Knoll, Andrew H. 2003. *Life on a Young Planet: The First Three Billion Years of Evolution on Earth.* Princeton, NJ: Princeton University Press.

Koch, Christof. 2004. *The Quest for Consciousness: A Neurobiological Study.* Englewood, CO: Roberts & Co.

Laski, Marghanita. (1961) 1968. *Ecstasy: A Study of Some Secular and Religious Experiences.* New York: Greenwood Press.

Leary, Timothy. 1968. *The Politics of Ecstasy.* New York: Putnam.

Leuba, James H. 1929. *The Psychology of Religious Mysticism.* New York: Harcourt Brace.

Levinthal, Charles F. 1988. *Messengers of Paradise: Opiates and the Brain.* New York: Anchor Press/Doubleday.

Lewis-Williams, J. David. 2002. *The Mind in the Cave: Consciousness and the Origins of Art.* London: Thames & Hudson.

————, and David Pearce. 2005. *Inside the Neolithic Mind: Consciousness, Cosmos and the Realm of the Gods.* London: Thames & Hudson.

Lindbergh, Anne Morrow. 1955. *Gift from the Sea.* New York: Pantheon.

Louv, Richard. 2005. *Last Child in the Woods.* New York: Algonquin Books.

Lovelock, James. 1988. *The Ages of Gaia: A Biography of Our Living Earth.* New York: W.W. Norton.

Maclean, Norman. 1976. *A River Runs through It and Other Stories.* Chicago: Univ. of Chicago Press.

Mandell, Arnold J. 1980. "Toward a Psychobiology of Transcendence: God in the Brain." Chap. 14 in *The Psychobiology of Consciousness,* edited by Julian M. and Richard J. Davidson. New York: Plenum Press.

Margulis, Lynn, and Dorian Sagan. 1986. *Microcosmos: Four Billion Years of Evolution from Our Microbial Ancestors.* New York: Summit.

————. 2001. "The Beast with Five Genomes." In *Natural History* 110 (June) 38–41.

Marshall, Paul. 2005. *Mystical Experiences with the Natural World: Experiences and Explanations.* Oxford: Oxford University Press.

Martin, Graham Dunstan. 1990. *Shadows in the Cave: Mapping the Conscious Universe.* London:Arkana/Penguin.

————. 2005. *Does it Matter? The Unsustainable World of the Materialists.* Edinburgh: Floris Books.

Maslow, Abraham H. 1964. *Religions, Values, and Peak Experiences.* Columbus: Ohio University Press.

Masson, J. Moussaieff. 1980. *The Oceanic Feeling: The Origins of Religious Sentiment in Ancient India.* Boston: Reidel.

Matthiessen, Peter. 1978. *The Snow Leopard.* New York: Penguin Books.

Melville, Herman. (1851) 2001. *Moby Dick, or the Whale.* 150th Anniversary Edition, New York: Penguin.

Mercer, J. Edward. (1913) 1997. *Nature Mysticism.* London: George Allen. Repr., Kila, MT: Kessinger.

Milton, Kay. 2002. *Loving Nature: Toward an Ecology of Emotion.* London: Routledge.

Mitchell, Edgar, with Dwight Williams. 1996. *The Way of the Explorer: An Apollo Astronaut's Journey through the Material and Mystical Worlds.* New York: Putnam.

Mitchell, R. G. Jr. 1983. *Mountain Experience: The Psychology and Sociology of Adventure.* Chicago: University of Chicago Press.

Mowry, Robert D. 1997. *Worlds within Worlds: The Richard Rosenblum Collection of Chinese Scholars' Rocks.* Cambridge, MA: Harvard University Art Museums.

Muir, John. 1994. *The Wild Muir: Twenty-Two of John Muir's Greatest Adventures.* Yosemite National Park, California: Yosemite Association.

Murchie, Guy. 1978. *The Seven Mysteries of Life: An Exploration in Science and Philosophy.* Boston: Houghton Mifflin.

Murphy, Michael, and Rhea A. White. 1995. *In the Zone: Transcendent Experience in Sports.* New York: Penguin/Arkana.

Myers, F. W. H. (1880) 1929. *Wordsworth.* London: Macmillan.

Nabhan, Gary Paul. 1977. *Cultures of Habitat: On Nature, Culture and Story.* Washington, DC: Counterpoint.

Nabokov, Vladimir. 1951. *Speak, Memory: A Memoir.* London: Gollansz.

Naess, Arne. 2002. *Life's Philosophy: Reason and Feeling in a Deeper World.* Translated by Roland Huntford. Athens, GA: University of Georgia Press.

Newburg, A. B., E. G. d'Aquili, and V. P. Rouse. 2001. *Why God Won't Go Away: Brain Science and the Biology of Belief.* New York: Ballantine.

Newhall, Nancy. 1963. *Ansel Adams.* San Francisco: Sierra Club.

Nicholsen, Shierry Weber. *The Love of Nature and the End of the World: The Unspoken Dimensions of Environmental Concern.* Cambridge, MA: MIT Press.

Nietzsche, Friedrich W. (1896) 2000. *Ecce Homo.* New York : Penguin.

Olson, Sigurd F. 1956. *The Singing Wilderness.* New York: Alfred A. Knopf.

Orr, David W. 1992. "For the Love of Life." In *Conservation biology* 6 (December).

Ortega y Gasset, Jose. 1972. *Meditations on Hunting.* New York: Scribner's.

Parsons, William B. 1999. *The Enigma of the Oceanic Feeling: Revisioning the Psychoanalytic Theory of Mysticism.* New York: Oxford University Press.

Peat, F. David. 1987. *Synchronicity: The Bridge between Matter and Mind.* New York: Bantam.

———. 2000. *The Blackwinged Night: Creativity in Nature and Mind.* Cambridge, MA: Perseus Publishing.

Peirce, Charles S. 1934. *Collected Papers.* Cambridge, MA: Harvard University Press.

Pert, Candace B. 1999. *Molecules of Emotion: The Science behind Mind-Body Medicine.* New York: Touchstone.

Petersen, David. 2000. *Heartsblood: Hunting, Spirituality, and Wildness in America.* Washington, DC: Island Press.

Polanyi, Michael. 1966. *The Tacit Dimension.* New York: Doubleday.

Raine, Kathleen. "Nature: House of the Soul." In *Temenos* 9: 251–268, 1988.

Restak, Richard M. 2000. *Mysteries of the Mind.* Washington, DC: National Geographic Society.

Rezendes, Paul. 1998. *The Wild Within: Adventures in Nature and Animal Teachings.* New York: Jeremy P. Tarcher/Putnam.

Richardson, Robert D. 1995. *Emerson: The Mind on Fire.* Berkeley: Univ. of California Press.

Rolland, Romain. (1929) 1984. *The Life of Ramakrishna.* Calcutta: Advaita Ashrama.

Rosenblum, Richard. 2001. *Art of the Natural World: Resonances of Wild Nature in Chinese Sculptural Art.* Boston: MFA Publications.

Roszak, Theodore. 1992. *The Voice of the Earth.* New York: Simon and Schuster.

———, Mary E. Gomes, and Allan D. Kanner. 1995. *Ecopsychology: Restoring the Earth, Healing the Mind.* San Francisco: Sierra Club.

Roth, Harold D. 1999. *Original Tao: Inward Training (Nei-yeh) and the Foundations of Taoist Mysticism.* New York: Columbia University Press.

Rowley, George. (1947) 1970. *Principles of Chinese Painting.* Princeton, NJ: Princeton University Press.

Russell, Bertrand. 1919. *Mysticism and Logic, and Other Essays.* New York: Longmans, Green.

Schneider, Stephen H., and Penelope J. Boston. 1991. *Scientists on Gaia.* Cambridge, MA: MIT Press.

Service, Alastair, and Jean Bradley. 1979. *Megaliths and their Mysteries.* New York: Macmillan.

Shepard, Paul. 1999. *Encounters with Nature.* Washington, DC: Island Press.

———. 1996. *Traces of an Omnivore.* Washington, D.C.: Island Press.

———. 2003. *Where We Belong: Beyond Abstraction in Perceiving Nature.* Athens: Univ. of Georgia Press.

Sinnot, Edmund W. 1950. *Cell and Psyche: The Biology of Purpose.* Chapel Hill: Univ. of North Carolina Press.

———. 1966. *The Bridge of Life: From Matter to Purpose.* New York: Simon and Schuster.

Slovic, Scott. 1992. *Seeking Awareness in American Nature Writing: Henry Thoreau, Annie Dillard, Edward Abbey, Wendell Berry, and Barry Lopez.* Salt Lake City: Univ. of Utah Press.

Stace, W. T. 1961. *Mysticism and Philosophy.* London: Macmillan.

Stallknecht, Newton P. 1958. *Strange Seas of Thought: Studies in William Wordsworth's Philosophy of Man and Nature.* Bloomington: Indiana University Press.

Stange, Mary Zeiss. 1997. *Woman the Hunter.* Boston: Beacon Press.

Stevens, Anthony. 1993. *The Two Million-Year-Old Self.* Carolyn and Ernest Fay Series in Analytical Psychology 3. College Station: Texas A&M University Press.

———. 2004. *The Roots of War and Terror.* London: Continuum.

———, and John Price. 1996. *Evolutionary Psychiatry: A New Beginning.* London: Routledge.

Stevens, Wallace. 1997. *Wallace Stevens: Collected Poetry and Prose.* New York: Library of America.

Storr, Anthony. 1988. *Solitude: A Return to the Self.* New York: Free Press.

Suchantke, Andreas. 2001. *Eco-Geography: What We See When We Look at Landscapes.* Translated and with an introduction by Norman Skillen. Great Barrington, MA: Lindisfarne Books.

Suzuki, David, with Amanda McConnell. 1998. *The Sacred Balance: Rediscovering Our Place in Nature.* Amherst, NY: Prometheus Books.

Swedenborg, Emanuel. 1749–1756. *Arcana Coelestia.* Repr., New York: American Swedenborg Printing and Publishing Society,1853–1857.

Taylor, Eugene. 1990. "William James on Darwin: An Evolutionary Theory of Consciousness." In *Psychology, Perspectives and Practice.* Edited by Sheila M. Pfafflin. *Annals of the New York Academy of Sciences,* 5.

———. 1996. *William James on Consciousness beyond the Margin.* Princeton, NJ: Princeton University Press.

———. 1999. *Shadow Culture: Psychology and Spirituality in America.* Washington, DC: Counterpoint.

———. 2002. *The Spiritual Roots of James's* Varieties of Religious Experience. Introduction: Section One, to Routledge Centenary Edition of *The Varieties of Religious Experience.* London: Routledge.

Taylor, Gordon Rattray. 1979. *The Natural History of the Mind.* New York: Dutton.

Teilhard de Chardin, Pierre. (1955) 1999. *The Human Phenomenon.* New edition and translation by Sarah Appleton-Weber. Brighton: Sussex Academic Press.

Thomas, Lewis. 1974. *The Lives of a Cell: Notes of a Biology Watcher.* New York: Penguin.

Thomashow, Mitchell. 2002. *Bringing the Biosphere Home: Learning to Perceive Global Environmental Change.* Cambridge, MA: MIT Press.

Thoreau, Henry David. 1984. *The Collected Poems of Henry Thoreau.* Edited by Carl Bodes. Baltimore: Johns Hopkins University Press.

———. 1985. *The Portable Thoreau.* New York: Penguin.

———. 1962. *The Journal of Henry D. Thoreau.* Edited by Bradford Torrey and Francis H. Allen. New York: Dover.

———. 1964. *Collected Poems of Henry Thoreau.* Edited by Carl Bode. Baltimore: Johns Hopkins University Press.

Todhunter, Andrew. 2000. *Dangerous Games.* New York: Doubleday.

Tompkins, Peter, and Christopher Bird. 1973. *The Secret Life of Plants.* New York: Harper & Row.

Tuan, Yi-Fu. 1974. *Topophilia: A Study of Environmental Perception, Attitudes, and Values.* Englewood Cliffs, NJ: Prentice-Hall.

Turgenev, Ivan. Undated. *A Hunter's Sketches.* 1847–1851. Classics of Russian Literature. Moscow: Foreign Languages Publishing House.

Underhill, Evelyn. 1915. *Mysticism and War*. London: J. M. Watkins.

Vaitl, Dieter et al. 2005. "Psychobiology of Altered States of Consciousness." In *Psychological Bulletin* 131, no.1, 98–127.

von Essen, Carl. 1996. *The Revenge of the Fishgod*. Forest Dale, VT: Paul S. Eriksson.

von Wright, Georg Henrik. 1986. *Vetenskapen och Förnuftet: Ett Försök till Orientering* [Science and rationality: An attempt at orientation]. Borgå, Finland: Söderström.

———. 1988. "The Myth of Progress." In *Architecture and Cultural Values*. Report of the 4th Alvar Aalto Symposium. Jyväskylä, Finland: Alvar Aalto Symposium.

———. 1993. *Myten om Framsteget* [The myth about progress]. Stockholm: Bonnier.

Walsh Roger N. 1990. *The Spirit of Shamanism*. Los Angeles: Jeremy P. Tarcher.

Washburn, Sherwood, and C. S. Lancaster. 1968. "The Evolution of Hunting." In *Man the Hunter*, edited by Richard B. Lee and Irvin DeVore, 293–300. Chicago: Aldine.

Wilson, Edward O. 1984. *Biophilia*. Cambridge, Mass.: Harvard University Press.

———. 1998. *Consilience: The Unity of Knowledge*. New York: Alfred A. Knopf.

———. 2002. *The Future of Life*. New York: Knopf.

Wittgenstein, Ludwig. (1922) 1994. *Tractatus logico-philosophicus*. Translated by D.F. Pears and B.F. McGuiness, with an introduction by Bertrand Russell. Repr., London: Routledge.

Wordsworth, William. 1988. *The Essential Wordsworth*. Selected and with an introduction by Seamus Heaney. New York: Ecco Press.

Zaehner, Robert Charles. 1957. *Mysticism Sacred and Profane: An Inquiry into Some Varieties of Praeternatural Experience*. Oxford: Clarendon Press.

———. 1972. *Zen, Drugs, and Mysticism*. New York: Pantheon Books.

Zajonc, Arthur. 1993. *Catching the Light: The Entwined History of Light and Mind*. New York: Bantam Books.

Zohar, Danah. 1990. *The Quantum Self: A Revolutionary View of Human Nature and Consciousness Rooted in the New Physics*. In collaboration with Ian Marshall. London: Bloomsbury.

———, and Ian Marshall. 2000. *SQ: Spiritual Intelligence, the Ultimate Intelligence*. London: Bloomsbury.

Illustrations

"I Become a Transparent Eyeball," page 18; *Transparent Eyeball*, a caricature of Ralph Waldo Emerson by Christopher Cranch (c1836–1846).

"A quantum eyeball's viewpoint," page 19; from *Mind in Nature: Nobel Conference 1981*, Richard Q. Elvee, ed., New York: Harpercollins, 1982.

"William James and Paul Ross," page 70; *William James and Paul Ross*, (1887), [fMS Am 1092] are used by permission of the Houghton Library, Harvard University, and Bay James.

"Fechner's wave-scheme of consciousness," page 98; Published by Gustav Fechner in *Elemente der Psychophysik* (1860).

"William James's stream of thought," page 102; William James's "stream of thought," Principles of Psychology (1860).

"William James's stream of thought (revised by the author)," page 103; by the author, after William James "stream of thought."

"Brain and limbic system" images, page 106; by the author.

"Mi Fu bowing to the rock," page 143; Yu Ming (Chinese, 1994–1935): *Mi Fu at Stone Worship*, early twentieth century, 62.1 x 33.2 cm.; gift of Robert Hatfield Ellsworth, in memory of La Ferne Hatfield Ellsworth, 1986.

Index

CARL FRANÇOIS VON ESSEN, M.D., was born in 1926 and raised in Northern California. After medical studies in California and Sweden, he practiced and taught in the United States, India, and Switzerland and served the World Health Organization in Sri Lanka and Zimbabwe. Throughout a long professional career spanning the globe, he devoted available time to exploring the natural world and pursuing his passion for angling. He is also the author of *The Revenge of the Fishgod: Angling Adventures around the World.* Carl von Essen now lives in Cambridge, Massachusetts, with his wife, the author, anthropologist, and Jungian analyst Manisha Roy.